The Autism-Friendly Guide
to Self-Employment

THE
AUTISM-FRIENDLY
GUIDE TO
SELF-EMPLOYMENT

Robyn Steward

Jessica Kingsley Publishers
London and Philadelphia

First published in Great Britain in 2021 by
Jessica Kingsley Publishers
An Hachette Company

1

A CIP catalogue record for this title is available from
the British Library and the Library of Congress

ISBN 978 1 78775 532 1
eISBN 978 1 78775 533 8

Printed and bound in Great Britain by TJ Books Limited

Jessica Kingsley Publishers' policy is to use
papers that are natural, renewable and recyclable
products and made from wood grown in sustainable
forests. The logging and manufacturing processes
are expected to conform to the environmental
regulations of the country of origin.

Jessica Kingsley Publishers
Carmelite House
50 Victoria Embankment
London EC4Y 0DZ

www.jkp.com

MIX
Paper from
responsible sources
FSC
www.fsc.org   FSC® C013056

Contents

This book is split into parts and chapters, and each part has an icon.

Acknowledgements

Thank you to Keith Bates, Cary Griffin, Dave Reid, Peter Smith and Tony McLean for being peer reviewers for this book.

Thank you also to James Potter and Polly Raymond, Nicholas, who inspired the idea, Kindling Studios, Creativity Explored, Greg and Anlor, Matt of Stutterking Bakery and his family, the Edmonton focus group, Renate Burwash, Alex and his mum, Shane Leith, Liz Wenn, Madge, Jeremy, Niche Comics, Lisa, Sean, Adam, Ros, Vicki, Judy Napper, my mum and dad, Majbritt of Oliz in Denmark, Heart n Soul, Sarah Jane and Ben.

Introduction

About the author

Welcome to this book.

My name is Robyn. I am autistic. I have tried traditional employment; it didn't work for me. I've been self-employed for over ten years.

You can read more about what I do at www.robynsteward.com.

Who is this book for?

This book is for you if you want a basic and (I hope) simple to understand guide to coming up with self-employment ideas, working out how much to charge, getting paid, formal business set-up, negotiating the benefit/welfare system, and understanding your tax obligations. You will also read about how to keep the records needed to run a business, as well as stories of autistic people who are self-employed from all over the world, and links to further information relevant to the UK, USA, Canada, Australia and New Zealand. However, this book is not a complete guide – more of a starting point.

Research for this book

Before writing this book, I talked to many autistic people, via surveys, e-mail and face to face. I also contacted people who support people to start businesses, and read lots of business books.

Why did I write this book?

I wrote this book to complement the other great business

books out there. Here is a list of some interesting books on starting a business/self-employment:

- *Going Self-Employed: How to Start Out in Business on Your Own – And Succeed!* by Steve Gibson
- *Survival Skills for Freelancers* by Sarah Townsend
- *SYOB/Start Your Own Business* by Rieva Lesonsky and the staff of *Entrepreneur* magazine
- *Make It Happen: The Prince's Trust Guide to Starting Your Own Business* by The Prince's Trust
- *Company of One: Why Staying Small Is the Next Big Thing for Business* by Paul Jarvis
- *Who Moved My Cheese? An Amazing Way to Deal with Change in Your Work and in Your Life* by Spencer Johnson
- *Start with Why: How Great Leaders Inspire Everyone to Take Action* by Simon Sinek
- *Contagious: Why Things Catch On* by Jonah Berger
- *The Business Book: Big Ideas Simply Explained* by Dorling Kindersley
- *SOLO: Survival Guide for Creative Freelancers* by Palle Schmidt
- *Big Ideas...for Small Businesses: Simple, Practical Tools and Tactics to Help Your Small Business Grow* by John Lamerton.

Common misconceptions about self-employment

I appreciate that self-employment might seem very scary. I think when people think about self-employment, they imagine...

- becoming ineligible for benefits/welfare
- having to quit other forms of employment
- taking great risks, e.g. financial risk.

Being self-employed does not have to result in any of these
scenarios.

How this book is organised

You can read the chapters of this book in any order. I have used
some symbols for country-specific information or to highlight
particular kinds of information/activities.

Symbol	Country
Bulldog	UK
Eagle	USA
Moose	Canada
Kangaroo	Australia
Kiwi	New Zealand

Other symbols used in this book

	Symbol	Meaning
	Question mark	Word explanation
	Signpost	Links to further information such as web links or books
	Magnifying glass	Suggestions for keywords for a web search, e.g. Google or Bing
	Pen writing	Activity: something for you to try
	Script (like a film script)	Things you can say or write in particular situations
	Speech bubble	Quote from research participant or my personal perspective
	Tick	Indicates where you should add a tick

At the end of each chapter is a list of 'action points' that you should have completed while working through the chapter. Put a tick next to each action point when you have completed it.

Common business words

Before we go any further, here are some words that are used commonly in business.

 Self-employed: This describes a person who is responsible for getting their own work, paying their own taxes, invoicing, sales, holidays and sick pay/ allowance. This is different to being an employee, whose employer would be responsible for these aspects.

Sometimes a person who is self-employed is described as running a business, a freelancer or a contractor. (NOTE: Contractor could be used in the context of being employed by a business.)

 Business: In the context of this book, a person or persons who do things to earn money, e.g. a person who builds houses runs a business building houses.

 Service: A service is something that can be done to or for someone else, such as gardening, massage or computer repair.

 Product: Something that can be sold to and used by the customer – i.e. the customer owns the product.

 Client/customer: Someone buying something – this could be a service such as paying for a haircut or goods.

 Goods: A word sometimes used to describe something physical you can buy such as an apple or a bag of compost.

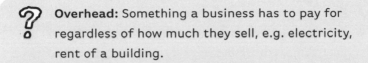

Overhead: Something a business has to pay for regardless of how much they sell, e.g. electricity, rent of a building.

Making a loss/losing money: This means to spend more money than you get back from a self-employment/business activity.

Making a loss

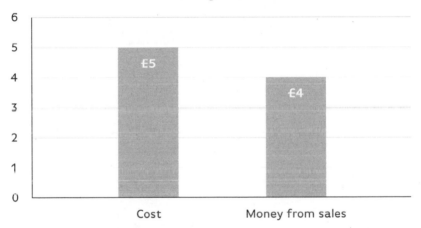

EXAMPLE OF MAKING A LOSS

If you spent £5 making cupcakes and you sold 20 cakes for 20p (20 pence) each, you would get £4 (400 pence), £1 less than the amount of money you spent on making the cakes.

This would mean you had made a loss of £1.

INGREDIENTS COST £5   20 CUPCAKES

Profit: This means to get more money back than you spent buying or making the product in a self-employment/business activity. Gross profit is the money left after you have paid for making or buying the product and have sold it to a customer. You subtract overheads like lighting, heating and internet from your gross profit to give you net profit. Net profit is the money you keep and the money you pay personal tax on.

Making a profit

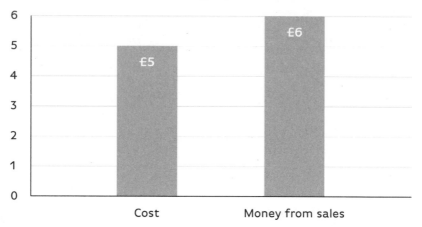

EXAMPLE OF MAKING A PROFIT

If you sold the cupcakes for 30p (30 pence) each you would get £6 (600 pence), so you would make a profit of £1.

How I calculated this
30p x 20 (you have 20 cupcakes and sell them for 30 pence each)

= £6

Deduct £5, which is the money you spent making the cupcakes

= £1: this is your profit.

 Breakeven point: This is when you didn't lose any money, but you did not make a profit.

Break even

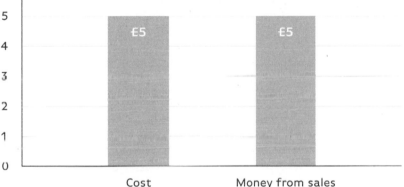

EXAMPLE OF BREAK EVEN

The break-even point of the cupcake business would be where you took £5 from the sale of your cupcakes and that is how much money you spent making the cupcakes. This would be the case if you sold 20 cupcakes for 25p (25 pence) each.

Each example does not include the time taken to make the cupcakes (sometimes described as labour, as you would physically be making something): they are just an illustration of the terms used.

Activities within this book

There are plenty of practical activities for you to do in this book. You don't have to write in the book – you can just use a notepad and pen/pencil. You also don't have to do all the activities; just do the ones you feel will benefit you. Feel free to adapt activities to meet your own needs or situation.

Disclaimer about tax, laws and benefits/welfare

Check with someone with experience of the relevant legislation in your country or investigate the laws yourself (see Section 3.5, page **53** for in-person help). Much of the available information on benefits, welfare/pensions, taxes and so on is general information. Everyone's situation is unique, so you need to find out how it applies to you.

Good luck

If it doesn't work out the first time, try and try again. But remember that to try again doesn't mean just repeating what you did before that didn't work. Evaluate what didn't work, change it, and try again. You may have to go through this process a few times.

PART 1

Get Ready for Self-Employment

Estimated time to read Part 1: 1 hour 40 minutes

Aims: In Part 1 you will identify what your needs are as a self-employed person.

1

What Is Self-Employment?

I.I What does being self-employed mean?

Being self-employed means that rather than working for someone else's company, business or organisation, you have your own company/business/organisation. This could be just you on your own, or it could be you and several other people working together. Some people start a business with their family, for example 'Johnson and Sons', and some people start a business with a friend. You can do this formally using types of businesses like partnerships or limited companies – see Section 15.2, page **208** for more information.

When you are self-employed you can choose when you work and what work you do, and all the money you earn goes into your bank account (either your personal account or a business bank account). You are responsible for paying your own tax. You are your boss! Running a business (being self-employed) does have a lot of responsibilities, which I will cover in this book.

NOTE ON BANK ACCOUNTS: Pretty much all of the peer reviewers for this book emphasised the need for caution when using your own bank account for business purposes. You must make sure you keep a record of money that goes into your bank account and out of your bank account for business purposes so that you can separate personal spending and income with business spending and income. Where possible it is advisable to use a business bank account.

Self-employment is something many autistic and non-autistic people do, and you can do it too.

I.2 What does self-employment look like?

Here are some examples of what self-employment can look

like, and what the aims of the people running the businesses might be. This is not an exhaustive list.

- Someone on a fixed income (e.g. benefits/pension) doing something they enjoy.
- A person or group of people living in supported accommodation wanting to do something meaningful.
- A person who has built up skills in employment and wants more control over their work life.
- A parent who starts a business for/with their child.
- A person who sees a need in the community.
- A person who needs to create a portfolio or get experience within a particular industry.

Portfolios

 Portfolio: A portfolio is a document or series of documents (which could be digital) that contains examples of work a person has done.

Photographers and artists may have photos of their work or illustrations in their portfolio, while proofreaders and copy-editors may have testimonials/quotes (feedback) from past clients as well as some excerpts from their work. A garden landscaper might have photos of work they have done in people's gardens (you must make sure you have permission to share photos of other people's belongings). A portfolio might also contain development work, for example illustrations/diagrams of prototypes of a product.

You need to adapt your portfolio for what your industry/sector is. You might also have a website, as well as business cards that have images of your work on one side (moo.com make double-sided business cards which allow you to have a selection of images on the back of each one).

1.3 What are your barriers to self-employment?

 Barrier: In this context it means something that gets in the way of doing something, e.g. not having a car could be a barrier to being able to run a minicab business.

Write a different barrier that you think you have on each brick in the wall below (you don't need to fill in every brick). Refer back to your list of barriers as you read this book. Cross off the barriers when you overcome them.

Examples

- Not sure about what tax I would need to pay.
- Worried I won't make enough money.
- Not sure how to get customers.
- Find social interaction with people I do not know difficult.

BARRIERS

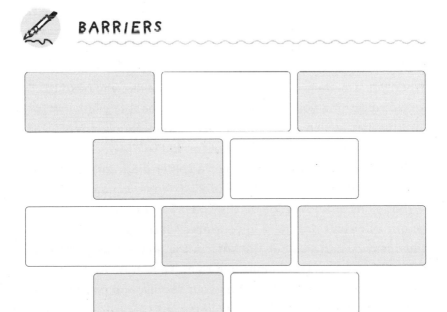

1.4 Supported self-employment

If you need help in several aspects of running a business, or are supporting someone who will need help in several aspects, you might find supported self-employment is a good option. Supported employment is still something that is evolving in many countries, but details of two helpful organisations are given below.

UK

BASE: British Association for Supported Employment	www.base-uk.org

CANADA

CASE: Canadian Association for Supported Employment	www.supportedemployment.ca

1.5 Your network

When you are starting a business it can feel like you need to know everything yourself, but you can ask people you know for information, advice and practical help – think family, friends and local businesses. It may be helpful for you to draw a 'mind map' (sometimes called a brainstorm or a spider diagram) of who is in your network. Think of your family, friends, acquaintances – what skills or knowledge do they have? Thinking further, what businesses are there in your area? Think about not just the ones you can see, but the ones in the phone book, on Yelp, Google Maps, etc. (You might like to make two mind maps: one for personal connections such as your family, and one for local businesses. Alternatively, you could make lists or draw pictures to represent the different people and businesses.)

Example mind map

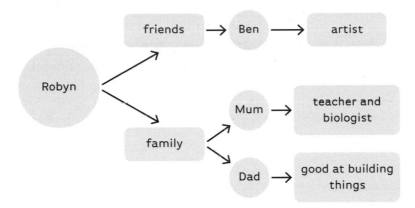

 **MIND MAP**

1.6 Review

In this chapter you will have identified what self-employment is, and what you think your barriers to self-employment might be. You will also be able to name people within your network, so you know you're not alone.

ACTION POINTS

Tick in the box when you have completed each action point.

1. List the barriers you face when thinking about exploring self-employment. ◯

2. Make a mind map/list or drawings of your network – this could include family and friends. ◯

2

Activities to Increase Your Self-Esteem

Estimated time to read this chapter: 25 minutes

Many autistic people who contributed to the research for this book stated that self-esteem was a barrier to starting a business. This chapter has a few activities that may help increase your self-esteem.

2.1 Things you have done in your life so far

To get to the point of reading this book, you have done stuff. You have probably learnt to read (or listen to audio books), but you may also have gained qualifications such as GED or GCSEs. You may have no formal qualifications, but you still have done stuff in your life.

On the next page, list 5–10 things you have done so far in your life that have taken effort, practice or commitment. They don't have to be academic things; they could relate to sports, caring for animals, and so on.

Examples
- I made baked goods, e.g. cakes.
- I completed a computer console game.
- I wrote a short story.
- I trained my puppy.

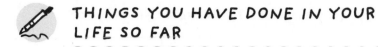

THINGS YOU HAVE DONE IN YOUR LIFE SO FAR

1. ....

2. ....

3. ....

4. ....

5. ....

6. ....

7. ....

8. ....

9. ....

10. ....

2.2 Why do you want to be self-employed?

In the next activity write why you would like to be self-employed, and draw a picture to illustrate it. Try not to be too general, for example 'I want to make a million' (this is probably the wrong book for you). Instead say what you want a million for, for example 'I want to buy my own home' or 'I want to buy a car'. Cut the picture out (or take a photo of it on your phone and print it out, or photocopy it) and stick it somewhere you will see it every day, for example on a mirror, bathroom door or wardrobe door.

Examples
- I don't want to work for a company that does not share my values.
- I want to share my art with other people.
- I want to be able to work around my children's schedule (school drop-off/pick-up, etc.).

WHY YOU WOULD LIKE TO BECOME SELF-EMPLOYED

· ·

· ·

· ·

· ·

· ·

2.3 Words that describe you or words other people use to describe you

- Has anyone ever complimented you?
- Has anyone said kind words about you?
- Has anyone described you favourably?
- Is there anyone you'd feel comfortable asking what words they'd use to describe you? (This could be a friend or a family member.)
- Are there positive words you would use to describe yourself?

If you answered yes to any of the above questions, write down the qualities people mentioned on the next page.

Other ways of sourcing words that describe you

- Ask friends using social media or e-mail.
- If you have a lot of friends/followers on social media, such as Facebook, who you actually interact with (liking their posts, sharing posts, commenting, etc.), you could ask them, or post a short survey on a survey website such as SurveyMonkey, Google Forms or SmartSurvey. (The advantage of a survey website is that people can comment anonymously.)
- You could ask something like this:

 'I am exploring self-employment, and would like to ask what skills and attributes other people see in me. I am not trying to ask for praise – I just want to understand how others see me.'

Or:

 'What positive attributes/qualities do you see in me?'

Personality tests

Any personality quiz or test is bound to have flaws, since it is trying to generalise the whole human population, which is almost undoubtedly not going to work because there are many varieties of people.

However, doing the '16 Personalities' test, which is based on the well-known Myers-Briggs personality types, and reading through the results may help you to identify your strengths if you do not have anyone to ask. You can find it at www.16personalities.com.

POSITIVE WORDS USED TO DESCRIBE YOU

. . . .

. . . .

. . . .

. . . .

. . . .

. . . .

. . . .

. . . .

. . . .

. . . .

2.4 Trial and error

Most people have to try some things several times before being able to do it right. This is sometimes known as trial and error.

List five things that you have had to try several times before getting it right or being able to do it consistently. (You may be able to list more than five.)

Examples

- Riding a bike: Fell off lots and now I can ride a bike.
- Baking scones: My first scones were a bit burnt and misshapen.

✎ TRIAL AND ERROR LIST

....

....

....

....

....

....

....

....

....

....

2.5 Review of lists

Now you should have four lists:

- Things you have done in your life so far.
- Why you would like to be self-employed.
- Positive words used to describe you.
- Trial and error list.

As you go through the process of exploring (and hopefully trying) self-employment, if you start to doubt yourself or get lost in the detail of things that aren't working out right, use the resources you just created to try and put some perspective on what's happening, and understand that right now it is only a small part of your life. If this doesn't work out, it's OK! At least you tried, and hopefully you learnt from it.

2.6 Positive affirmations

One other thing you could do with these lists is write some affirmations. Affirmations are statements that you can use to tell yourself that you can do things. Below are some examples. You could try saying each one five times when you wake up each day.

Examples
- I am recognised by other people to be thoughtful.
- I can learn from my mistakes, like the time I learnt to ride a bike.
- In my life I have travelled by train alone.
- I am going to use self-employment to have control of when and where I work.

POSITIVE AFFIRMATIONS LIST

I am recognised by other people to be...

. . . .

. . . .

. . . .

(from the 'Positive words used to describe you' list)

I can learn from my mistakes, like the time I...

. . . .

. . . .

. . . .

(from the 'Trial and error list')

In my life I have...

. . . .

. . . .

. . . .

(from the 'Things you have done in your life so far' list)

I am going to...

. . . .

. . . .

. . . .

(from the 'Why you would like to be self-employed' list)

2.7 Resources to help with self-esteem

Exploring Depression, and Beating the Blues by Tony Attwood and Michelle Garnett.

Flip It: How to Get the Best Out of Everything by Michael Heppell.

2.8 Review

In this chapter we covered some activities that may help you to increase your self-esteem, and what you can do if you are fearful of failure.

ACTION POINTS

Tick in the box when you have completed each action point.

1. Things you have done in your life so far list. ☐

2. Why you would like to be self-employed list. ☐

3. Positive words used to describe you list. ☐

4. Trial and error list. ☐

5. Positive affirmations list. ☐

3

Self-Management

3.1 What expectations should you have when starting a business?

Most people's experience of self-employment is that it takes time to make a profit and to get work coming in regularly. There are of course some people who become very successful very quickly, but that isn't most people's experience!

Self-employment often involves learning new things. Be prepared to try things, but if you find you need extra support with anything, this is OK.

With the help of this book and using other resources, write below what you expect to be able to do yourself and what you need help with. (You might not know what you'll need help with right now, so you could come back and fill this list in at another time.)

Examples
- I expect I will be able to serve customers.
- I expect I will need help with answering phone calls.

 ## WHAT DO YOU EXPECT OF YOURSELF?

I expect I will be able to...

. . . .

. . . .

. . . .

. . . .

. . . .

I expect I will need help with...

. . . .

. . . .

. . . .

. . . .

. . . .

3.2 Training and learning

 'I would advise people to find (part-time) work in the industry you aim to be self-employed in. That will be good training and will introduce you to others in the industry.' (**Research participant**)

If you are employed the business/organisation you work for may offer training; some tell their employees how many hours of training they should do each year. This could be in subjects like first aid training or public speaking, and they will have informal opportunities for feedback on their work from colleagues, customers and managers, as well as formal feedback through appraisals (this varies from employer to employer but all of these opportunities help the employee to do their job better).

When you are self-employed you are responsible for your own training and personal/professional development. The good news is you can tailor it to your needs.

Many of the autistic people I spoke to did 'training', though it may look very different to what you might imagine training to be like.

EXAMPLES

Matt of Stutterking Bakery wants to open his own cafe. To learn how cafes operate, he is going to get a part-time job in a cafe.

Shane, a web developer, read books about communication to help him learn to communicate with his clients.

Recently I identified that I didn't know much about search engine optimisation (SEO), and also wanted to make my website easier to navigate. I did some free online courses on Google Digital Garage. I then adapted my website and reviewed the results. (**Robyn**)

 SEO (search engine optimisation): Ways to make a website more visible on search engines such as Google.

I suggest reviewing your development at least once a year. You may want to do it more often. Identify things you don't know about but that may help you run your business, along with ideas about places you may find training and development, and write them below.

Examples

- Networking
- Public speaking

Places you may find training and development

- In-person help providers (see Section 3.5, page **53**)
- Chamber of commerce
- Unions
- Federations, guilds and societies
- YouTube or Vimeo
- Google Digital Garage
- (learndigital.withgoogle.com/digitalgarage)
- OpenClassrooms (openclassrooms.com/en)
- Coursera (www.coursera.org)
- Mastermind groups

WHAT WOULD YOU LIKE TO LEARN ABOUT THAT WOULD HELP YOU RUN YOUR BUSINESS, AND WHO PROVIDES THE RELEVANT TRAINING?

....

....

....

....

....

....

....

....

....

....

 Mastermind group: Some people prefer peer learning and may set up a mastermind group, which is a group of similarly experienced self-employed people who meet frequently to support each other (sort of like a work support group).

You could form a virtual mastermind group via Facebook, Skype or other social media platforms, and/or local autism groups/organisations, networking groups, etc.

The concept of mastermind groups was introduced by Napoleon Hill in his book *The Law of Success*, although I first read about them in Palle Schmidt's book *SOLO: Survival Guide for Creative Freelancers*.

 Peer: Someone who is at the same level as you. For instance, pupils in your class at school were your peers, whereas the teachers were not your peers because they had authority, were teaching you and were older than you.

3.3 Ways to manage your energy

During the research for this book, people talked a lot about the importance of managing energy. For many people, this was very difficult. In the next few pages there is information and activities that may help you to manage your energy.

Energy accounting

Maja Toudal is an autistic woman who developed a system for energy accounting. You can find her website here: www.majatoudal.com.

Energy accounting is when you work out:

- how much energy different activities in your daily life use
- what your energy threshold per day is (this may fluctuate during the course of a year)
- what boosts your energy.

You can then manage your energy 'a bit like a bank account', says Maja Toudal.

Spoon theory
Christine Miserandino, on her website ButYouDon'tLookSick. com, first blogged about spoon theory in 2010. Spoon theory is a way of representing your energy with spoons (as a metaphor).

Each day, if you sleep well, you will have a certain number of spoons. Some tasks cost/use spoons (energy), and some things help you gain spoons. What costs and gains spoons will be individual to each person, as will how many spoons a person starts with each day.

 SPOONS

On the next two pages there are two spoons: a plus (+) spoon and a minus (−) spoon.

Draw or write on the plus spoon things that help you gain spoons, for example sleep.

Draw or write on the minus spoon what costs spoons, for example socialising.

You could also colour code the activities; for example, red activities cost most spoons, amber costs a few spoons, and green costs even less.

If spoons don't work for you, consider whether a battery might be a better metaphor: what charges your battery (gives you energy), and what uses a lot of energy/runs your battery down?

If metaphors are not helpful for you, you can skip this activity.

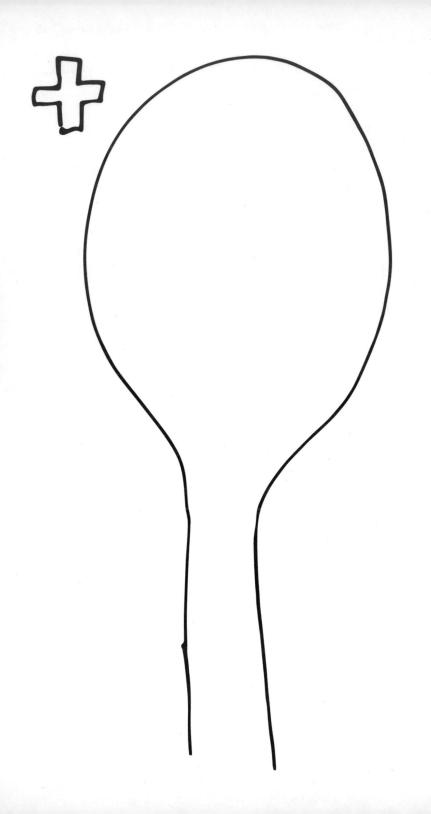

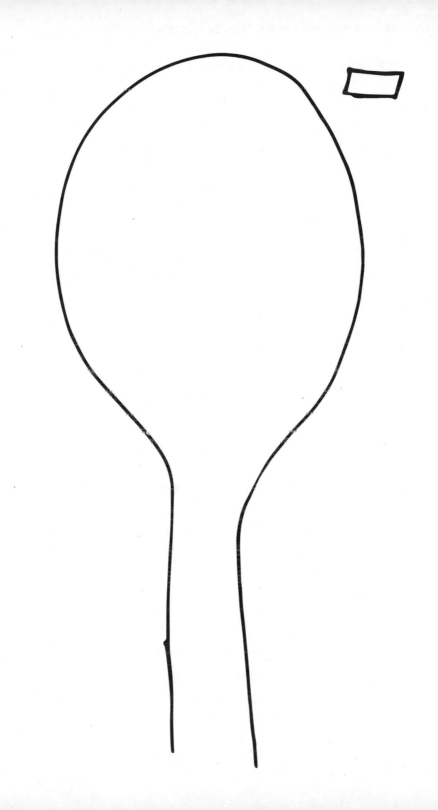

3.4 What are boundaries?

Boundaries can be physical, like a wall or fence, or non-physical, like rules. For example, if someone didn't like being hugged, then being hugged would be a boundary.

Self-employed people need boundaries to try to avoid burnout and becoming overwhelmed, whilst also looking after their customers and making sure their business meets all its legal requirements.

There are different kinds of boundaries – for example:

- professional boundaries, e.g. not giving out personal information, such as the date you were born, to customers
- legal boundaries, e.g. you are legally required to fill in (or get someone to fill on your behalf) a self-assessment tax return
- wellbeing boundaries, e.g. taking days off to avoid being overwhelmed
- financial boundaries, e.g. not spending too much or too little on a piece of work
- communication boundaries, e.g. only communicating via e-mail
- pricing boundaries, e.g. having a limit on how much discount you will give the customer/client
- time boundaries, e.g. how many hours you will spend doing something.

 'Scheduling time off, or "rest days", into my diary makes it less likely I burn out.' (**Research participant**)

 Burnout is when a person is physically and emotionally exhausted (definition from www.helpguide.org).

It is important to set professional boundaries. Sometimes boundaries are set by an organisation. For example, the British Association for Counselling and Psychotherapy have protocols (rules) for counsellors and therapists. They have a professional register, and if you did not follow the protocols you would be taken off the register.

EXAMPLE

Many autistic people feel passionate about what they do for work, and charge less than other people. However, if a business does this for a long time, it will make it difficult to keep the business going. In addition, it makes it difficult for other businesses to survive because other business owners/self-employed people will struggle to pay their bills. If you charge less than other similar businesses, then customers will start expecting a cheaper price, which is unsustainable for the business.

Knowing the market rate and charging that rate for your product or service is really important.

 Market: In the context of self-employment/business, 'market' can mean:

- the people willing to buy a product or service
- people in a geographical area, like a town (e.g. Springfield)
- a virtual market, like a business online selling to people in the UK, or it could be more specific, such as the UK market for fashion for women aged 18–24 in sizes 8–16 shopping online.

 Market rate (sometimes known as the going rate): A market rate is the common price people buying a product or service pay. This can vary between geographic/online locations. It can also vary depending on the sector your business operates in. Sometimes when a business is selling to another business they may offer a discount.

 Sector: A sector is a category of a business, e.g. the hospitality, arts or retail sectors.

Boundaries for customers

You need to set boundaries about what people are buying. For example, if you are asked to proofread a document, the person paying you may decide that they are going to add more pages to the document. If you have been clear that the cost you quoted the client was for the original word count they sent you, then they must pay for the extra time it will take you to do the extra work. Having arrangements in writing is important to clarify expectations for you and your client/ customer.

Personal boundaries

 'Getting stuck on one detail that probably isn't that important to the project but seems that way at the time to the detriment of the actual project.'
(**Research participant**)

If you focus on very small details in a project too much, you may find that you are not able to look after yourself. For example, not getting enough sleep or leisure time would not be sustainable for most people over a long period of time, both in terms of physical and mental health. It is important to understand what you need to do to give yourself a good quality of life; for example, do you need to work when your children are at nursery/school, or do you need to be able to pay rent or save for a mortgage? How many hours' sleep do you need? How much money do you need to buy the food you like?

It is also important that you find out what is important to the client and set yourself limits within which to work. For example, you should set yourself a suggested amount of hours to work each week, or an estimated time for each part of the project, even though you might find to begin with your estimates are not accurate. You will learn by experience how to estimate how long a piece of work will take – this is also important to know for how much you should ask to get paid for your work; even if you are not charging per hour you still need to decide if you can get the work done in the time and money available and earn enough to pay your bills and meet your own and your family's needs.

If you are working in a context where tendering/commissioning is common (e.g. the arts or professional development training), then how much money is available and how much you are comfortable working for (how much you will get paid), and any costs incurred by the project, will influence whether you apply or do not apply for a commission/tender. I am not trying to say that you should never concentrate on the details of a project, but just that you should make sure that you don't overdo it.

How can you formally create boundaries?
The formal way of setting boundaries is to use a contract, agreement or constitution (see page **222** for more information).

Constitution: A constitution is a set of rules that are agreed by a group of people who are in charge of something. For example, the Constitution of the

United States sets out the principles on which other laws are based, or a business constitution would refer to the way the business is run, such as how profits are split and so on.

Boundaries for your own wellbeing

You need to set limits on how much work you will commit to doing, and how many hours you will work. Self-employed people often describe the amount of work they get as 'feast or famine'.

 Feast or famine: This is a metaphor that means self-employed people either have a lot of work on or not enough work.

It can be easy to say yes to all offers of work because you are worried about the future, or enjoy work. This is something which every self-employed person has to learn to manage, though it can take many years to learn to do this. Having a limit of hours you'll work per week may be helpful for your own mental and physical wellbeing.

Also, the amount of communication and type of communication you have with your clients may need boundaries. For example, a boundary could be not speaking to clients on the phone. Sometimes you may break your own rules for very short periods of time. For example, in November 2020 I was doing an evaluation for an online festival and I worked more hours in a six-week period than I would normally, but this was because I then had two weeks off so the hours worked vs. not worked evened out.

Do you have any ideas about what might be some good boundaries for you? If so, write them down below.

Example

Have a work phone and a personal phone (these could both be mobile/cell phones), and turn the work phone off when you're not at work.

WHAT ARE YOUR BOUNDARIES?

. . . .

. . . .

. . . .

. . . .

. . . .

. . . .

. . . .

. . . .

. . . .

3.5 Where can you get support to start a business?

Most countries offer in-person help for starting a business. This could include mentoring, training sessions, information and advice. Below are some links to sources of information.

UK

The LEP (Local Enterprise Partnership) Network: A partnership between local authorities and businesses	www.lepnetwork.net/growth-hubs
England National Business Support Helpline	Telephone: 0800 998 1098 enquiries@businesssupport helpline.org
Scotland Find Business Support Scotland	Telephone: 0300 303 0660 Textphone: 0800 023 2071 https://findbusinesssupport.gov. scot
Wales Business Wales Helpline	Telephone: 0300 060 3000 Contact form: https:// businesswales.gov.wales/ contact-us
Northern Ireland Invest Northern Ireland	Telephone: 0800 181 4422 enquiry@investni.com www.investni.com

USA

Small Business Administration	www.sba.gov
America's SBDC: Nationwide network of Small Business Development Centers	https://americassbdc.org
Association of Women's Business Centers	www.awbc.org
EARN: Employer Assistance and Resource Network on Disability Inclusion Lists Vocational Rehabilitation Agencies by state	https://askearn.org/state-vocational-rehabilitation-agencies

CANADA

Canada Business Network (CBN)	www.canada.ca/en/services/business.html
Community Futures (for rural areas)	https://communityfutures canada.ca
Futurpreneur Canada For ages 18–39	www.futurpreneur.ca
Startup Canada	www.startupcan.ca

AUSTRALIA

SelfStart	https://jobsearch.gov.au/selfstart

NEW ZEALAND

Regional Business Partner Network	www.regionalbusinesspartners.co.nz/#section-contact
Business information on the New Zealand government website	www.business.govt.nz

Other sources of information

- Libraries
- Federation of Small Businesses
- Trade unions
- Chambers of commerce
- Online courses: often these are free and can be found on platforms like Coursera, OpenClassrooms and Google Digital Garage
- University business incubator programmes
- Local charities (not-for-profits) offering training and information

Making business support work for you

In the UK people who help people start a business are sometimes called advisors; in the USA they are called counsellors.

You have a choice! You can keep switching advisor/counsellor until you find someone who understands you. One thing to know is that sometimes people are not compatible with each other. This has nothing to do with being autistic – non-autistic people are also sometimes not compatible with certain people. If working with a particular person is not working out for you, you can say something like...

 'I appreciate your help. I was wondering if it would be OK to seek opinions from other counsellors/advisors working here?'

3.6 What is mentoring?

 Mentoring is when a person with experience or knowledge of something (in this context being self-employed) supports someone with less experience. Mentoring usually involves talking in person, over the phone or via the web (video or text based) – whatever works for you and your mentor.

Mentoring was a theme that came up a lot in the research for this book. In many countries there are mentoring schemes available that are either free or low cost. Don't be put off because a mentoring scheme is not autism specific. Mentors do not have to have worked with autistic clients before for the mentor/mentee relationship to be successful. If the mentor is willing to learn and understand what you can and can't do, they can still help you. If it doesn't work out with you and a mentor, you can ask for someone different.

WHERE TO FIND A MENTOR

UK

Mentorsme.co.uk: Online gateway for business mentoring	www.mentorsme.co.uk
Prince's Trust: Support for starting a business	www.princes-trust.org.uk/help-for-young-people/support-starting-business

USA

Real World Scholars (RWS): For young people	www.realworldscholars.org
US Small Business Administration (SBA)	www.sba.gov/local-assistance/find
SCORE: Helps small businesses through mentoring and education	www.score.org
Association of Women's Business Centers	www.awbc.org

CANADA

Futurpreneur Canada	www.futurpreneur.ca/en/mentoring
Startup Canada	www.startupcan.ca

AUSTRALIA

Business Enterprise Centres Australia	https://becaustralia.org.au/about
New Enterprise Incentive Scheme (NEIS)	www.employment.gov.au/self-employment-new-business-assistance-neis

NEW ZEALAND

Business Mentors New Zealand   www.businessmentors.org.nz

3.7 Accountability

 Accountability means taking responsibility for the things you have to do.

> **EXAMPLE**
>
> If a security guard was sat at the front of a store playing on their phone and let a thief steal from the store, to hold the security guard to account would be to say something like: 'Your job was to monitor the security of the store.' If the security guard was behaving in a fully accountable way, perhaps they would offer to give the store the money lost out of their wages because they had not fulfilled the responsibilities of their job.

When you're self-employed you have to be accountable to yourself; it is a lot of responsibility. Personally, I find this less pressure than being employed, as I don't have to guess what someone else is thinking or expecting.

Yes, being self-employed does mean you can do what you want when you want, but if you don't get work done in time, if you're not actively seeking new clients/customers and improving your business, then you may get into difficulty.

How can you hold yourself accountable?
Business advisor: Use a business advisor/counsellor to help set your goals and give you feedback on your progress.

Groups: Join a mastermind group (see Section 3.2, page **41** for more information on mastermind groups).

Non-direct challenges: A direct challenge would be something like someone asking you if you have done what you said you would do this week. Some people may not find this helpful. You may prefer to go to events where you will see the same group of people who will ask how things are progressing, such as a regular networking breakfast.

Reward: You might use an activity as a reward. For example, you might arrange to go to the cinema but only allow yourself to go if you have met targets/goals you have set for yourself (make sure the targets are achievable and you are firm with yourself – don't go if you've not met your target).

If you don't need anyone else putting pressure on you
If, like me, you put a lot of pressure on yourself in general, you may find self-employment works well and that you do not need support with being accountable.

3.8 Work needs check-in

Identifying what you need, or what environments/situations make working more difficult, is important. There should be no shame in having needs, identifying them, and doing as much as possible to get them met. Below is a checklist which you can add to help you start thinking about your needs. You may want to do this activity on a separate piece of paper. The headings and questions below are just suggestions and not supposed to be exhaustive.

ACCESS/NEEDS AUDIT

Sensory

What kind of sensory environment do you need? ◯

Do you prefer to stay in one place during your workday? ◯

Do you prefer moving around, e.g. walking or going to different offices/shops? ◯

Do you like to be outside? ◯

Do you like to be inside? ◯

Do you need no distractions when you are working? ◯

Social interaction frequency, intensity and type

Do you like meeting lots of different people? ◯

Do you prefer working with just a few people? ◯

Do you prefer to spend your workday alone? ◯

Do you enjoy being around people who are passionate about the same things as you? ◯

Do you enjoy building relationships with people over long periods of time, or do you prefer short bursts of interaction with lots of different people? ◯

Communication: How do you communicate?

Do you have specific communication needs? ◯

Are you able to verbally speak all the time? ◯

Do you have times when you have to communicate in a different way? ◯

Do you hate the phone? ◯

Do you prefer text-based communication? ◯

Do you like to communicate face to face? ◯

Focus

Do you 'hyperfocus' for periods of time rather than your energy being distributed over your workday? ◯

Do you prefer to work in the morning? ◯

Do you prefer to work in the afternoon? ◯

Expectations and demands

Do you need a clear task with deadlines and expectations? ◯

What helps you to manage the demands of others?

. . . .

. . . .

. . . .

. . . .

. . . .

3.9 Review

In this chapter you learnt about ways to think about managing your energy and boundaries as well as thinking about training and development opportunities that may look quite different for self-employed people. You also learnt where you can get help starting a business, what mentoring is and possible sources of mentoring.

ACTION POINTS

Tick in the box when you have completed each action point.

1. Write down what you expect of yourself and what you expect you will need help with.   ☐

2. Identify areas where you think you would benefit from training or learning opportunities.   ☐

3. If it is helpful, fill in the spoons pictures.   ☐

4. Write or draw any ideas you have about boundaries in relation to being self-employed.   ☐

5. Have a look at the websites relevant to your country for in-person help with self-employment.   ☐

6. Look at the sources of mentoring support.   ☐

7. Fill in the access/needs audit and add in categories and items as needed.   ☐

3.10 Optional experiment to give you an idea of what it could feel like to be self-employed

Before you leave this chapter, consider doing a little experiment. Find something in your home you no longer need that is in good condition and that you own, and put it on

Craigslist, Jiji, Gumtree, eBay or whatever your local classified online ad service is.

If you do not want to give out your address or go to someone else's house, choose a small item to sell and either post the item to the buyer (perhaps you are best using eBay to help facilitate this) or meet in a public place like a train station or busy street. See what it feels like to sell something.

Maybe meeting a stranger feels scary. Maybe going to the post office is difficult.

Or if you're like me, you'll get a big grin on your face, not because you've made a big profit, but just because you sold something, which is a move forward.

If this feels like too big a jump, what about asking your friends, family or people in your neighbourhood if they would pay you to walk their dog, clean their car or do another task you feel confident doing? Or you could do the task with a sibling or friend. This is how many businesses start, and whilst you might not stick with this task as your self-employment activity, it is still experience.

PART 2

Risks

Estimated time to read Part 2: 40 minutes

Aims: In Part 2 you will learn what a risk is and make a risk map, identify common risks of self-employment and learn how to reduce those risks.

4

Introduction to Risk

4.1 What is a risk?

A risk is a possibility that something might happen. Normally the word 'risk' is used when talking about negative things that might happen.

You can usually do things that will reduce the likelihood of the risk happening. This is sometimes described as 'mitigating a risk'.

EXAMPLE

One risk of riding a bicycle is falling off and injuring your head.

Here are some ways to mitigate the risk:

- wearing a cycle helmet
- participating in training sessions on how to ride safely
- reading books about cycling safety/Highway Code
- seeking guidance from people who are more experienced at cycling.

Traditional employment is not without risks, for example being made redundant or being fired from your job, needing to geographically relocate, job role changing, change of boss or manager, and not getting on well with them.

Using risk maps

It is normal to be worried about the risks of something, especially if it's something you have never tried before. It is mostly possible to mitigate risk. Draw/write a mind map (or if you prefer a list or some pictures) of the risks you think self-employment might have for you. You might not be able to think of any right now, but as you read this book it may be helpful to come back to this. You can use the risk map list to work out what your risks are and then use this as a starting place for further research.

Optional: You could grade your risks, for example from 1 to 5, where 1 = very unlikely/little risk and 5 = very likely/high risk.

Example risk map

RISK MAP

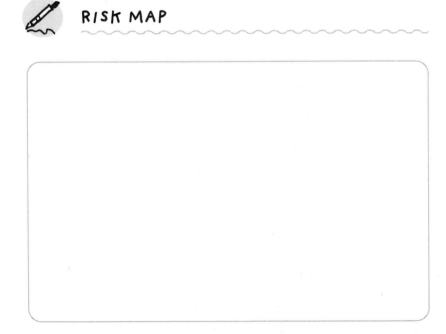

In the rest of Part 2, I have tried to address common risks people identify when thinking about self-employment.

4.2 Review

In this chapter, we have looked at what a risk is and how to draw a risk map.

ACTION POINTS

Tick in the box when you have completed each action point.

1. Understand the meaning of 'risk'. ⃝

2. Learn about risk maps. ⃝

5

How to Mitigate Risks to Benefits/ Welfare/Pension Entitlement

Estimated time to read this chapter: 15 minutes

Losing, or a change in entitlement to, benefits/welfare, pension or social security is a common concern. This risk is manageable. This chapter gives some strategies to help mitigate this risk.

Summary of potential ways to mitigate risks

- Be aware that not all benefits will be affected by your employment status.

  Some benefits/welfare/pensions are not means tested (i.e. not affected by how much money you earn). In the UK, examples of non-means-tested benefits are PIP (Personal Independence Payment), DLA (Disability Living Allowance) and the state pension.
- Set up a business within an organisation and/or share resources.
- Use different business structures.
- Limit your profit.
- Find out your entitlement to benefits/tax credits.
- Research, research, research!
- Check when you need to register as self-employed.
- Work with an organisation.
- In the UK, manage the Universal Credit minimum income floor.
- In the USA, decide if you are going to use a representative payee (see page **77**), PASS (Plan to Achieve Self-Support), PESS (Property Essential to Self-Support) or an ABLE (Achieving a Better Life Experience) Account (see page **81**).

5.1 Setting up a business within an organisation and/or sharing resources

Some businesses are set up within, or in collaboration with, a business or organisation such as a school or care provider. Sometimes this is done informally. There are rules that need to be followed to use this as a strategy. Other people have done it, so it's not impossible.

> **EXAMPLES**
>
> **Spotlight Brewing: Example of formally working with an organisation**
> Spotlight Brewing is a small brewery which is in the same location as a care/group home for people with learning disabilities (intellectual disabilities). The brewery is mainly run by people with learning disabilities who are residents at the care home.
>
> www.spotlightbrewing.co.uk
>
> **Made by Brad: Example of informally working with an organisation**
> Brad is autistic and has an intellectual disability. His mum and dad set him up a business building flat-pack furniture (Brad loves building things). They came to an arrangement with the day programme Brad attends that the staff would take him to customers' houses to assemble their flat-packs.
>
> https://madebybrad.com
>
> **A Clean Sweep: Example of using a business structure**
> A Clean Sweep was set up in 1995 and is a co-operative, which means it is owned and managed by its members, who all have an equal say in how it is run. The members

of A Clean Sweep are its employees, who are people with learning difficulties. Each employee gets an equal say in how the business is run and can control how much they earn personally. This means they can make sure their individual earnings won't affect their benefits.

   www.acleansweep.org.uk

5.2 Using different business structures

The type of structure your business has (see Chapter 15 for more information on business structures), and the rules locally, will determine how government systems treat you. For example, as a person (as opposed to a business), you can receive benefits. Some business structures allow your business to be a separate entity (and so does not receive benefits). If this seems confusing, it's OK – I have written about this in more detail in Chapter 15.

5.3 Limit your profit

You can limit your profit by using business expenses to help your business grow (see Section 16.4, page **228** for information about expenses). This means that your benefits are less likely to be affected.

5.4 Find out your entitlement to benefits/tax credits

You might find becoming self-employed entitles you to more benefits or additional benefits. Most governments incentivise getting paid work because it means people will pay taxes, which in turn fund public services. Work is also a protective factor for mental illnesses, and in countries where the government provides mental health support, if people need less mental health support, this again saves the government money.

5.5 Research, research, research!

Research the rules around benefits and self-employment – don't just assume it won't work. Use the in-person help links in Section 3.5, page **53** to seek the advice of people who know how the system works, as sometimes what is written on a website is slightly different to how it works in real life.

 Search online for your country + 'what income is considered when calculating welfare/benefits'.

5.6 Check when you need to register as self-employed

Most countries will let you sell something you make or do as a hobby. In many countries, a hobby is classed as a business when you start making a profit. While you try your ideas out, you could buy extra materials to make more product, or buy in more expensive materials, so you won't make a profit and there will be little, if any, effect on your benefits/welfare entitlement. Obviously, this is not a long-term solution, but it gives you a chance to try out an idea with less risk.

 Search online for your country + 'difference between hobby and business'.

Profit: When you have more incoming money than outgoing money.

5.7 Working with an organisation

In the creative industries, some people join organisations like art studios, which can help manage sales of your work, and therefore manage the profits that would affect your benefits/welfare. The money from the sales of your work could go towards paying for the studio/workspace, for buying art supplies, and for paying for assistants and equipment.

EXAMPLE OF WORKING WITH AN ORGANISATION: CREATIVITY EXPLORED

Creativity Explored is an art studio in the Mission District in San Francisco. Most of their artists receive SSI and/or SSDI (Supplemental Security Income/Social Security Disability Insurance). In the USA you can get what is known as a 'representative payee'. This could be a family member, or an organisation that offers 'representative payee services' (see the box that follows).

Creativity Explored takes a percentage of sales, with the rest of the money going to the artist. Artists on SSI or SSDI have to formally tell the social security department about any extra money they earn. Some artists choose to donate their work to Creativity Explored. Money from the sales of artwork is spent on the artists, through teaching/support equipment and opportunities to explore new mediums.

 www.creativityexplored.org

Representative payee services

In the USA a representative payee is a person who can receive social security monies on your behalf, pay your bills, etc. if you are unable to do this yourself. There are agencies/organisations that offer representative payee services, often run by The Arc (a US national not-for-profit organisation that supports people with learning and developmental disabilities). Some Arcs have a separate agency they work with to manage this service.

5.8 Managing the Universal Credit minimum income floor

In the UK, if you get Universal Credit and are expected to work you will have to navigate the minimum income floor (some people receiving Universal Credit are not expected to work). The minimum income floor is the amount of money the government thinks you should be earning and is calculated as minimum wage multiplied by 35, because they expect you to work 35 hours a week and get the minimum wage (there are some people for whom this does not apply).

Being self-employed does not work in quite the same way as when you are employed because the amount of hours you work a week can vary a lot, as can the profit that you earn, so you may find it helpful to work out what your Universal Credit minimum income floor is and then work out how much this is each month. If your net profit (money that you have been paid for work minus expenses) is less than the minimum income floor, you won't get extra Universal Credit, but if your net profit is more than the minimum income floor you will be paid less Universal Credit. At the time of writing, the minimum income floor does not apply for the first 12 months after you register as self-employed.

Ways to control your net profit month to month
If you know you have a month without much work coming up, but the month before you have plenty of work, there are a few things you can do to be able to report earnings that meet the minimum income floor for both months. Invoices are useful here.

 Invoice: In the UK, this is a document that asks someone to pay for something. This could be products or services.

Invoices are usually used when people pay for the product/ service before or after they receive the product or service, or when one business is selling products or services to another business (you can find out more about invoices in Section 18.1, page **253**).

- The customer/client has payment terms you have both agreed, e.g. 30 working days. Stagger sending invoices to customers so that you'll get the money during the quiet month.
- Bill (invoice) customers at intervals of time. If you have regular clients, you could consider billing them each term/semester, or quarterly or annually.
- Many banks take 3–7 days for cheques to be processed. It is common for businesses to wait until the end of a week or month to pay in their cheques. If you pay a cheque in on the last day of the month, the money won't get into your account until the next month!

What if you don't do invoices?

(Note that in this context I am not talking about invoices given when a customer pays and receives their goods/services – I'm talking about when you write invoices before or after doing a piece of work/providing a good or a service.) Invoices are often used by businesses providing services. If invoices don't work for your type of business (often the case for businesses that sell products rather than services, e.g. a book shop), consider whether you can also offer services. For a book shop, for example, this could be a monthly book club subscription, book deliveries, a book shop club that gives people discounts on books, or the opportunity to attend free events such as authors reading from their books, or perhaps guest speakers speaking about topics covered in your book store.

If you're self employed and in the 'no work-related requirements' group, or the 'work-focused interview' or 'work preparation' group, then the minimum income floor won't apply. Further information on these groups is available here:

 www.turn2us.org.uk (search for 'Universal Credit' and the group you have been placed in)

5.9 Mitigating the risk of not having enough work or having a fluctuating income

- Work out how much money you need per month to cover rent/mortgage, bills, travel, food, etc. Sarah Townsend in her book *Survival Skills for Freelancers* describes this as your survival income.
- When you have a good month, save money.
- Use the benefit/welfare system to help you initially if you can.

- Research grants (see Section 8.7, page **121**). You might be surprised to learn what you can apply for.
- Look at what resources you have. For example, can you rent out your spare room via SpareRoom, Craigslist, etc.?
- If you have the energy and capacity, get part-time employed work, and work as a self-employed person part time.
- Accept that your income will be up and down for the first few years. Consider if you can add revenue streams (see Section 9.2, page **127**) that may offer predictability.
- Investigate tenders.

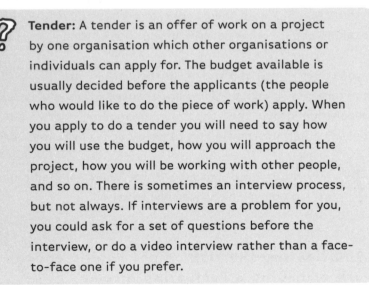

Tender: A tender is an offer of work on a project by one organisation which other organisations or individuals can apply for. The budget available is usually decided before the applicants (the people who would like to do the piece of work) apply. When you apply to do a tender you will need to say how you will use the budget, how you will approach the project, how you will be working with other people, and so on. There is sometimes an interview process, but not always. If interviews are a problem for you, you could ask for a set of questions before the interview, or do a video interview rather than a face-to-face one if you prefer.

- Investigate doing contract/freelance work for a larger company.
- If you are used to a regular amount of income each month, it can take time to adjust to self-employment, especially in the first few years.

USA

During my travels for the writing of this book, I found
that the USA has a number of initiatives that would
help people on low incomes wanting to become self-employed.
The information was difficult to find all in one place, and the
language often seemed overly formal. Here is a summary of
what I learnt.

- Vocational rehabilitation centres are a good source of
  information.
- The Arc may offer representative payee services or work
  alongside a not-for-profit who does this.
- Property Essential to Self-Support (PESS): This piece of
  legislation means that the Social Security Department
  will not take into account things you need to run your
  business, like money in the bank to pay bills, products
  you are going to sell, and sometimes parts of your home
  or land if they are used for business purposes when
  calculating your SSI (Supplementary Security Income)
  entitlement. 'Property' does not only refer to houses or
  land: it can mean college courses, pieces of equipment,
  etc. – basically, anything that costs money.
- A PASS (Plan to Achieve Self-Support) plan can help a
  person achieve an employment or self-employment goal.
  A PASS plan can mean that income or resources will not
  be considered by social security when calculating your
  entitlement to federal aid. You will need a separate bank
  account for your business monies.

  You can develop a PASS plan by downloading a form
  on the SSI website. You can also get help from state
  vocational rehabilitation centres to write your PASS plan.
  PASS plans usually last for a limited time, e.g. 3–4 years,
  and you have to demonstrate how you are progressing
  towards achieving your goal (identified in your PASS

plan). You can find more information about PASS in a PASS cadre — there is one in each state.

- ABLE (Achieving a Better Life Experience) Account: This is a special bank account that allows you to save for specific things without affecting your SSI. This includes basic living expenses, legal costs and education.

These organisations are useful for navigating the welfare system in the US:

Vocational rehabilitation centres list	https://askearn.org/state-vocational-rehabilitation-agencies
The Arc	www.thearc.org
Social Security website	www.ssa.gov/ssi
More information on PESS	https://secure.ssa.gov/apps10/poms.nsf/lnx/0501130500 or www.disability-benefits-help.org/glossary/property-essential-to-self-support
PASS cadre information	www.ssa.gov/disabilityresearch/wi/passcadre.htm
ABLE Account	www.able-now.com
Medicaid buy-in	www.health.ny.gov/health_care/medicaid/program/buy_in

EXAMPLE OF WORKING WITH THE BENEFIT SYSTEM

Wenn Lawson began his business in 1993, while on an Australian Single Parent's Pension, which later became a Disability Support Pension. Initially Wenn had to go to what is now called 'Centrelink' each week with his receipts, and his pension payment was altered according to how much he had earned. He found this very difficult to manage. He was assigned a social worker who was able to negotiate how often Wenn had to provide his receipts. Wenn got an accountant and began providing his accounts to Centrelink annually (see Chapter 17 for more information on accounting/bookkeeping).

Centrelink is the organisation that provides social security payments in Australia.

5.10 Risk of bankruptcy or losing your home

Bankruptcy sounds scary. It is a way of telling the government, banks and creditors and other people you owe money to that you have had problems managing money and can no longer afford to pay your debts.

Creditor: A person or company who lends you money or items (e.g. products to sell), e.g. a credit card company or another business who you are leasing equipment from.

Ways to avoid bankruptcy and losing your home:

- **Start small:** You don't have to be self-employed full time to begin with, and you don't have to spend loads of money to start a business.
- **Hobby vs business:** You might not be earning money at all at first, but just be getting experience, and therefore probably fit into the 'hobby' category. See Section 5.6, page **75** for further information about what is a hobby and what is a business.

- **IVA (individual voluntary arrangement):** If a person were to become bankrupt, there are special arrangements, such as an IVA, for paying back debt to creditors such as credit card companies. There are also many organisations who can provide assistance.

UK

These organisations can help in the UK:

StepChange Debt Charity	www.stepchange.org
Turn2us	www.turn2us.org.uk

5.11 Review

In this chapter we looked at ways of managing the risks around benefits and support entitlement and bankruptcy.

Different countries have different ways to manage the benefit system for self-employed people. Most countries also have a formal definition of a hobby and a business. It may be possible to test your ideas for self-employment with it still being considered a hobby.

ACTION POINTS

Tick in the box when you have completed each action point.

1. If you receive benefits/welfare/social security, investigate the rules about what income affects your benefit/welfare, and find organisations and advisors who know how the benefit system works in your country for self-employed people.

2. Research what your country considers a business or a hobby. ⃝

3. Investigate if there are government schemes providing financial assistance to people starting a business, or if there are other benefits that are available to you. ⃝

4. Research if there are any organisations you could work with, such as an arts studio. ⃝

6

Maintaining Your Health and Wellbeing

Estimated time to read this chapter: 20 minutes

6.1 How can pressure affect your mental health?

Think about any triggers you know you have, for example talking on the phone could trigger a panic attack for some people.

Think about what you can and cannot do on your worst days healthwise (e.g. if you have panic attacks).

- How often do these days occur?
- Do they happen as one-offs or in clusters, e.g. several days in a row?
- Is any recovery time needed?
- Is there anything that helps prevent them?
- Are there any things that prevent or reduce the likelihood of your health being affected, such as regular breaks or reduced working hours?

Below are some things to think about that might help you.

List business-related activities that you can do on your worst day. Some days you may be unable to do anything. That's OK. As you plan your business, try to choose self-employment ideas that would work for you. For instance, a copy-editor may have a few days to do a piece of work, whereas if you deliver training you have to deliver it on the day the client has specified.

Research support systems that can be put in place to help the business run when you are unable to work. It may be that you can write yourself some rules when taking bookings.

> **EXAMPLE**
>
> I try to avoid doing two full days' delivering training sessions consecutively (back to back) because I know

I'll be tired, and I schedule rest days in my diary. On a
rest day I do work, but I do the admin-type tasks, such
as bookkeeping or online research. My rest days are an
example of a support system.

Are you eligible for support? Or can you pay for it yourself?
There may be disability-specific schemes available for you,
such as the UK's Access to Work, which are designed to give
disabled people funds to pay for support at work if needed. In
the UK you may be entitled to a personal budget. A personal
budget is part of the UK system of social care which is aimed
at giving people more control on how allocated social care
money is spent to provide them with care and support. The
personal budget allows people to choose how they would
like to spend their time, as opposed to sending everyone
who requires support to a day centre. Personal budgets are
separate to access to work schemes and are administrated on
a local level by your local authority or council adult social care
department.

UK
The Social Care Institute for Excellence (SCIE)
can help support people according to their individual needs.
Their website provides information about personal budgets.

SCIE	www.scie.org.uk/personalisation/ introduction/rough-guide

Research other kinds of support
You may not want traditional worker-type support. If so,
consider things like a virtual assistant (VA) to do some of
the tasks you find difficult. There may be funding available
for people starting a business in your area (see Section 8.7,

page **121**) that could be used to pay for this kind of support. As you get more established you may be able to incorporate the fee of the person supporting you (see the example of Sarah Jane in Chapter 20) into the costs to your customers. This is perhaps more applicable if you are a service-based business.

 Virtual assistant: Someone you can pay to do things like phone calls, e-mails and admin, and help with marketing, who works virtually, i.e. from their home or office and not yours.

If you are a parent of someone who won't be able to manage money themselves, consider a trust.

EXAMPLE: MENCAP TRUST COMPANY

Mencap Trust Company is a British organisation which is set up to hold (look after) money left to the beneficiary (the person who the trust was set up to benefit) after the benefactor's death. It has a group of trustees whom the beneficiary (person who the money has been left to) can request funds from. The benefactor can stipulate rules around how the funds can be spent.

 www.mencaptrust.org.uk

6.2 Common ways people are taken advantage of

Being taken advantage of is a common concern for autistic people and their families, and sadly it is common for autistic people to be taken advantage of.

If you have low self-esteem it can be hard to know your worth, and also to feel you are worth standing up for.

Every human has value!!!! You have value! And if you don't feel worthy of doing it for yourself, know that not letting someone get away with taking advantage of you will make them less likely to try and take advantage of other people.

But pick your battles; sometimes you do have to let things go. It can be hard to work out what to let go, so seek advice from people you trust.

Sometimes autistic people (I know this from my own experience) can misinterpret things. Don't ignore how a situation makes you feel, and make sure you talk to a range of people you trust and get different opinions and perspectives on a situation.

If you run a business with another person(s), use a formal agreement, for example a partnership agreement, to do this. See Section 15.2, page **208** for more information.

Beware of pyramid schemes.

 Pyramid schemes are schemes where a person or business tells you that you will earn money if you recruit other people into the scheme. This is something to be avoided. The business is not really selling anything, and you will not make a profit.

 'Whenever I see anything for free, I am suspicious. I want to know how that business is making money, so I investigate and ask advice of others I trust.' (**Robyn**)

Avoid giving out sensitive information before checking the requesting person is not trying to scam you. Be on your guard if you get a phone call or e-mail from an organisation or person you do not know asking you for information, or to click a link and provide information or send back a form. Be particularly careful if they are asking for sensitive information, such as:

- bank details
- credit card numbers
- pin numbers
- any information relating to tax or business profits.

Sometimes, scammers will spoof a phone number, e-mail or web address. If someone calls you asking for sensitive information, even if you think you recognise the company or organisation, put the phone down, look up the company's number from a trusted source and call them back, if possible from a different phone. If they e-mail you, don't click on links in the e-mail, but go to their website directly. Don't return forms asking for sensitive information without checking that the form has legitimately been sent by the sender and the address has not been hacked.

Scam: This is when someone tries to trick you into giving them money or sensitive information that they can use to get money or forge documents.

Spoofing is when a person uses technology to send you e-mails/website links that look like they are sent from someone you know, or direct you to fake websites that look like ones you may want to visit.

Research what organisations/businesses you use, such as banks, will and won't ask for (this is usually on the websites of banks, credit card companies and similar organisations).

If you need to end a phone conversation, you can say:

'I'm sorry, I am unable to talk now. I will contact you myself shortly.'

Then put the phone down. Don't worry if you think this seems a bit rude; if the person is really from the organisation they say they are they won't mind, as they are aware that sometimes scammers impersonate their organisation.

Pressure selling

Sometimes a company (particularly those selling advertising) will call you and try to hurry you into buying something. This is called **pressure selling**. Examples of the things people say when they are using pressure selling techniques are:

- If you don't buy today it might cost you a lot more money.
- I need to send your ad to the editor today.
- You don't want to miss out on this amazing offer, do you?
- This offer is just for you. I am just about to leave for the day.

To end a pressure selling phone call, you could say:

 'Thank you for your call. I am going to consider your offer. If I want to proceed, I will call you. Please do not call me again.'

Then put the phone down. If the person calling asks what they could do to change your mind, just say 'nothing' and put the phone down.

Investigate motives when offered free stuff

Branded pens or pads of paper, or even stress balls, are quite common free merchandise from a company, and this marketing technique is harmless (see information on branding in Chapter 11). The motivation of the company that gives them is fairly obvious – they are advertising their company, and you can clearly see the branding. If a company says they are offering a free service or product, though, you must investigate the motives. Talk to others and see what they think. Use several review websites such as Google and Trustpilot to see what others have said about the business. Be aware that sometimes people pay others to write reviews about a business, so go through a number of them if you are concerned about a business's motives. Be very careful before accepting anything for free from a business/company when it's not obvious what the company gets out of it. Also, if there is no clear pricing structure or you do not understand the pricing information, do not engage with the company.

Avoid get-rich-quick schemes

You might see adverts that say things like 'work from home as much or as little as you like' and 'earn $1000 a week'. This kind of thing is usually a scam. Businesses are something you build up over time, not something that happens overnight (unless you have a unique idea and a bit of luck).

People not paying you

Keep records of goods and services you have sold, or where you have provided contracts and where applicable purchase orders. If a customer/client does not pay you and they signed a contract or purchase order, you can take this to a small claims court. This does not cost a lot to follow up (see Section 21.6, page **294**). You could also consider asking customers for deposits.

Be cautious of investment opportunities

Some investment opportunities can be genuine and profitable.

However, you should only invest money via someone you trust, and not through a cold e-mail or phone call. Don't make any decision in an initial phone call or e-mail exchange, and discuss it with people you trust. If you don't have people you trust who know about these things, see the advice for finding in-person help in Section 3.5, page **53**.

 Cold in this context, e.g. cold calling, means to contact someone you do not know when they haven't expressed an interest in your product/service.

This is what you can say to the person who called you:

 'Thank you, but any decision I make won't be done straight away. I will contact you if I want to proceed. Please don't contact me – I will contact you.'

Then put the phone down.

How can you tell if you should trust someone's business advice/information?
See Section 6.4, page **95** for guidelines.

6.3 Social isolation

Social isolation can be a common worry if you are autistic and find socialising difficult. It's understandable that you or those who support you may be concerned about this aspect of self-employment. Being self-employed does not have to be socially isolating, though, and sometimes you can prioritise quality rather than quantity of social interactions to make best use of your energy.

Ways to seek social interaction as a self-employed person
Small business networks can be a good way to meet. Local chambers of commerce and business federations, and small business growth hubs/organisations who help start-ups, are ways of meeting other business people.

 Start-up: New businesses in the process of being set up are sometimes called start-ups.

Some self-employment activities are social. For example, being a taxi driver involves talking to people (although most of the time your customers won't be your friends), and the interactions are short, which gives you time to recover (many autistic people find socialising tiring).

Self-employment can reduce the need to do small talk. Autistic people often find small talk, for example about the weather, or questions from co-workers when they don't want an honest answer (such as 'How are you?'), costs valuable energy. Doing what you are interested in for work can sometimes mean that social interactions seem less pointless.

Co-working spaces
Sharing a work environment with another person/business can help provide social interaction. See Section 8.3, page **114** for more information.

6.4 How to avoid inadvertently breaking the law

You need to be aware of your legal requirements as a business, and the laws about intellectual property/copyright/patents.

One source of information is trade unions. There are many

trade unions (e.g. the Musicians' Union and the Society of Authors in the UK) which you can join to access information specific to your industry.

There may be collectives, associations or clubs specific to your industry which can help you meet other like-minded people, both online or offline, who may have navigated through the same issues you are faced with (see Section 12.2, page **166** for links for unions).

 Intellectual property (IP) is a person's ideas/work.

 Copyright © is the right of the person who created a piece of work, e.g. music or book, to choose who can reproduce their work. Sometimes this is done through selling a customer a licence to use a particular piece of work, and sometimes copyright is given or sold to an organisation such as a book publisher or record company.

 Patent: A way of formally owning a design or technology, so others cannot copy it without permission. This is outside the remit of this book.

When choosing a **business name**, use Companies House (or your country's equivalent register of companies), an internet search engine, Facebook and other social media platforms, and a domain name search (see Section 13.3, page **183** for more information on domain names) to check no other business is using the business name you want to use. Whilst it is not generally illegal to use a name another business is using, it could cause you problems in the future, particularly if the business has trademarked (™) their name.

Trademark™: A trademark is a way of formally owning a name of a business or product or a way of doing something (sometimes called a method). If anyone else were to use the same name or copy your method that you have trademarked, then you could legally stop them.

Seek information on legal requirements on government websites and/or from local business centres or start-up support organisations (see Section 3.5, page **53** for details).

For laws relating to business monies, use a qualified accountant. See Section 17.3, page **240** for more information on accountants.

Note that knowing the different terms used in different countries is really important.

Guidance of whether advice is trustworthy
This list is not exhaustive but hopefully will be of use. A person or organisation is likely to be trustworthy if:

- they are attached to a government agency or a not-for-profit considered trustworthy, like the ones mentioned in this book
- they are not gaining in any way from offering advice to you
- they don't pressure you into making a choice.

6.5 You can learn from failure!

If you have done any reading about self-employment you have probably seen scary-looking statistics about how many businesses fail. As Jason Feifer, editor-in-chief of *Entrepreneur* magazine, says in his foreword to *SYOB/Start Your Own Business* (by Rieva Lesonsky and the staff of *Entrepreneur* magazine), the statistics do not give you all the detail. They do not account for a business closing when a business owner retires, or sells the business.

Jason goes on to say:

A business failing does not mean an entrepreneur has failed! To an entrepreneur a failed business is simply a data point. It teaches us what to do better next time. The greatest entrepreneurs in the world have cycled through many, many, many businesses before they hit upon their billion-dollar idea. At no point did these people give up. They didn't close one business, declare themselves a failure and go and get a desk job to toil away in obscurity. No, they dusted themselves off and started again.

6.6 Review

In this chapter we covered how you can plan a business around your health needs, as well as how to prevent social isolation and how to avoid being taken advantage of.

ACTION POINTS

Tick in the box when you have completed each action point.

1. If scripts for what to say in specific situations will help you, decide where to store them so you can access them quickly as needed.

2. Make a plan for avoiding social isolation.

PART 3

Developing Your Ideas

Estimated time to read Part 3: 50 minutes

Aims: In Part 3 you will start to develop some ideas about what you would like to do as a self-employed person, as well as make a plan for tackling the added responsibilities of being self-employed.

7

Ideas of What to Do as a Self-Employed Person

Estimated time to read this chapter: 20 minutes

7.1 How do you find something to make/sell/ provide as a self-employed person?

A good starting point is to think about the kind of work you want to do. Here are some things to think about (this is not an exhaustive list).

- Do you always want to go to the same place each day, or different places?
- Do you want to talk to customers for most of the day?
- Do you want to work by yourself?
- Do you want to work on a computer, or do you prefer to make/do things that are not computer based?
- Is there a particular industry/sector you want to work in?
- Do you like to problem solve?
- Do you want to provide a product or service to a particular group of people, e.g. older people, children?
- Do you want to speak to people via e-mail, video conferencing, the phone or face to face?

**Kinds of self-employment ideas
(sometimes called business models)**

- **Make** a product from scratch, e.g. food or writing.
- **Repair/restore** customers' things, rather than make things yourself, e.g. computer technician.
- **Buy and sell** products, either that you did not make, e.g. via a book shop, or things you did make.
- **Provide a service** such as gardening, window cleaning, dog walking or taxi driving.
- **Drop shipping:** If you do not have a lot of space, drop shipping is a popular way to get products made and sent to customers without needing the resources to make

or store the products yourself. For example, you could design a T-shirt printed with your artwork (or similar), and rather than doing the printing yourself, you would use a drop shipping company that would source raw materials (in this example T-shirts, ink and a printing company to print the T-shirts) and send the product to the customer.

- **Fulfilment by Amazon:** Some big online retailers (in this case Amazon) allow you to buy products and send them to the company's warehouse, then they will sell the products and arrange for them to be shipped to the customer. Amazon take a percentage of the price the product has been sold at for arranging all of the above, but it can be a good way of experiencing e-commerce with relatively low risk.

Many businesses will do a mix of business models.

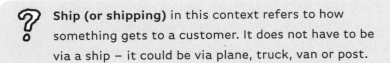

Ship (or shipping) in this context refers to how something gets to a customer. It does not have to be via a ship – it could be via plane, truck, van or post.

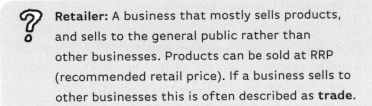

Retailer: A business that mostly sells products, and sells to the general public rather than other businesses. Products can be sold at RRP (recommended retail price). If a business sells to other businesses this is often described as **trade**.

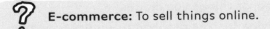

E-commerce: To sell things online.

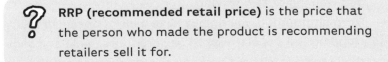

RRP (recommended retail price) is the price that the person who made the product is recommending retailers sell it for.

What motivates you?
What motivates you is an important question. Sometimes running a business is hard work and you don't always get to do the most enjoyable tasks. You need to feel motivated by the aims of your business. If what you decide to sell/make or provide does not motivate you, this could be a problem.

Work within your limits as a human
If you do not like to speak on the phone, you need to choose a business where you can usually avoid this. This applies to any of your needs, for example not working under fluorescent lights. Every human, whether they are autistic or not, has limitations – you do not have to feel bad about having limitations.

7.2 Think about how you will get work

As well as the work itself, you will also have to go out and find customers, or make it easier for them to find you. This is known as **marketing**. You need a business idea where the marketing is something you feel you can do.

7.3 Should you start a business based on your special/intense interests?

Having a business based around your interests can be a good idea. However, if you are someone whose interests often change drastically, and you find it hard to concentrate on past interests, then consider the interests you have had for a long time as a starting point for a business idea. Also think about what you will do if your interests change.

EXAMPLE

You might want to be a comic book illustrator. This is fine, but what happens if you ever become uninterested in comics? You could become an illustrator and start off doing comic books, but try to take on other illustration work that interests you to ensure you have a diverse portfolio and experience of different kinds of illustration. This will give you other options in the future if you need them.

7.4 Review your skills

Do you have the skills to do work based on your special/intense interests?

If you wanted to set up as a self-employed person doing computer repairs because you're interested in repairing computers, but you don't know *how* to repair computers, this would not be a business you could start straight away. You could, though, upskill and learn to build and repair computers by doing courses or work shadowing.

 Upskill: Learn additional skills.

 Work shadowing: Watching someone do a job to learn how to do it.

7.5 Should you start an autism-related business?

Sometimes at talks and training sessions, parents will tell me they think their child would be a great public speaker. Whatever your business idea, ask yourself:

- whether this is something you enjoy doing
- whether you either have the skills to do the work or are prepared to learn to do the skills
- whether the idea is compatible with your needs.

It is OK to just want to keep your special/intense interest as a hobby.

EXAMPLE: JEREMY SAMSON – PERSONAL TRAINER

Jeremy, who has Asperger's syndrome, lives and works in Melbourne, Australia. As a young child he got help from a strict exercise routine and change in diet, as well as playing sport, which had a positive effect on his mental and physical wellbeing. In his late teens, Jeremy studied health and fitness as a personal trainer and was working in gyms. One day a mother asked if her 14-year-old son with Asperger's could join. The gym was for adults only, but Jeremy stepped forward, explained that he could help as he had Asperger's himself, and suggested he could put a training programme together to help her son. Having completed further studies, Jeremy now works with all ages on the autism spectrum and has expanded his exercise programme to deliver one-to-one training.

The person-first language used in Jeremy's example is Jeremy's language preference.

7.6 How do people make self-employed income from music and performing arts businesses?

If you are wanting to earn money from making art of some kind, but particularly in the performing arts or music, you might think of members of orchestras, famous comics, actors on Broadway, TV or film, or famous musicians. Many people in the performing arts aren't earning anything like as much as famous artists, but there are lots of musicians who are earning enough. How do they do that?

Some of the ways people in the arts earn money are:

- gigs (informal entertainment events, e.g. comedy gigs or music gigs)
- selling merchandise, e.g. T-shirts they have designed (use websites like www.awsomemerch.com to create branded items)
- commissions (when someone asks you to create something)
- arts funding (remember to add your fee to your proposal)
- working on other people's art projects
- teaching other people
- promoting/curating
- selling music.

Different industries/sectors have different ways of getting paid

Different countries and professions have different ways of paying people. It is a good idea to join a large Facebook/social media group that relates to your industry. Ask questions there so you get a range of opinions and experiences (as things change) and get up-to-date information specific to your location. These groups also give you an insight into what other people are asking. Someone might say they are looking for someone with your skills for paying work.

Don't look at the groups as a marketing opportunity, but purely as a way of learning information.

Fee in this context is how much a person gets paid, e.g. the fee for a project is £1000. (For guidance on how much to charge, see Chapter 12.)

 Door split in this context means dividing the money that was paid by people coming to an event, e.g. 70/30 in the artist's favour would mean 70% of the money will be given to the artists (often divided per act) and 30% of the money is kept by the venue.

7.7 How do people earn money through the computer game industry?

During the research for this book, I met Shane Turner, a web developer, who is autistic and from Auckland in New Zealand (see Part 8, page **316** for his story). Whilst I don't want to promote the stereotype of autistic people all liking computers (there are many people who are autistic and like computers, but also many who do not), I do want to provide useful information. Shane, myself and Baz Armstrong, who is a senior lecturer for the computer games design degree at University Campus Oldham, helped compile this list. This isn't an exhaustive list.

Quality assurance (QA)/ playtester: Tests computer games and errors and gives feedback on playability, ease of navigation, etc.

Project manager/producer: Manages the production process, e.g. resources, deadlines, team interactions.

Computer programming: Could be in a specific area, e.g. user controls, game logic.

Concept designer: An artist who designs individual objects, environment elements, characters, creatures, vehicles, etc.

Designer: Designs the overall concept of the game, i.e. what's going to happen, the characters in the game, etc. May specialise in a specific area, such as how you move through the game, e.g. flying, running.

3D modeller: An artist who uses 3D modelling or 3D sculpting software to build the objects that the concept designer has designed. These models have to have the correct technical characteristics to be ready to work properly in the game. (Some concept designers specialise in textures/surfaces for virtual reality/augmented reality games.)

Technical animator/rigger: Puts bone structures into characters that enable the characters to be effectively animated, allowing for better movement, e.g. snails have a different body structure to humans.

Animator: Animates the characters so they move around in an appropriate way, e.g. run, jump, fight.

UX/user interface designer: Designs icons, buttons, on-screen information, etc.

Sound design: May include composition of music.

Sound engineer: A person who records sound. This could be sound effects, music or speech (e.g. actors performing a script).

Voice artist: Provides the voices for characters.

Scriptwriter: In this context, a person who writes a script about what will happen in a game.

Distributor: In this context, a company that sells games.

Proofreader: A person who checks the script and on-screen text for errors and corrects them.

Foley artist: Creates sound effects such as cars, footsteps, wind, etc.

LINKS TO UNIONS, ASSOCIATIONS AND FURTHER INFORMATION

INTERNATIONAL

TIGA: Network for games developers and digital publishers	https://tiga.org

UK

Ukie: Trade association for the UK's games and interactive entertainment industry	https://ukie.org.uk

USA

Entertainment Software Association (ESA)	www.theesa.com

CANADA

Entertainment Software Association of Canada (ESAC)	http://theesa.ca

AUSTRALIA

Interactive Games and Entertainment Association (IGEA)	https://igea.net

NEW ZEALAND

New Zealand Game Developers Association (NZGDA)	https://nzgda.com

See also www.screenskills.com/careers/job-profiles/games.

7.8 How do you know if something is a good business idea or not?

 'I also have a lot of ideas for self-employment and get really excited, but then I will completely lose confidence over the smallest thing.' (**Research participant**)

If an idea doesn't work, it doesn't mean you've completely failed. You will still have learned something. Most people don't get on a bicycle and start riding it and not fall off – they have to learn to balance, and steer using the handlebars (see the trial and error list in Section 2.4, page **35**). The same principle is true for running a business – you will learn by your mistakes and try again.

What can help guide your direction?

1. Research (see Chapter 10).

2. Meeting others who have done similar things.

3. Making a test product/service.

4. Work experience.

 Work experience: Trying out doing a particular kind of work.

When you start a business/become self-employed, does it have to be the one business idea you do for the rest of your working life?
No! It's really normal for people to do different business ideas. If they are a sole trader/proprietor (see Section 15.2, page **208** for information on sole proprietors), they might not change business, but rather change what they focus on.

7.9 Further sources of ideas

The Side Hustle School and their podcast, and the book *100 Side Hustles* by Chris Guillebeau.

The Creative's Guide to Starting a Business: How to Turn Your Talent into a Career by Harriet Kelsall.

How I Built This by Guy Raz.

 ## WHAT YOU COULD DO/SELL

You might find it helpful to draw pictures to represent your ideas. This could be a mind map or a list.

7.10 Review

In this chapter you read about strategies you can use to make a list or draw a mind map of things you could do as a self-employed person. Some people like to keep their special/intense interests just as a hobby, whilst others find it's a good idea to use them as the basis for an idea for self-employment. We also looked at why it is important to have some skills, or a plan to gain skills, to run a business.

We also explored how artists are are able to earn money as self-employed people.

In this chapter we also explored that the business idea you start with does not have to be the business idea you work on for the rest of your life.

ACTION POINTS

Tick in the box when you have completed each action point.

1. List or mind-map things you could sell/make/ service.

2. Decide why you want to try these ideas (it is best if you can find something you feel passionately about).

8

How to Start a Business with Limited Resources

Estimated time to read this chapter: 20 minutes

8.1 What is a resource?

 Resource: Something that you can use to do something. For example, a computer, printer, paper and ink cartridges are resources you might need to make a flyer.

Some businesses require particular resources, for example physiotherapists often require equipment and consulting rooms, or film makers may require use of particular computer software.

Not everyone has access to the resources they need when they become self-employed. In this chapter we explore ways to access resources. These suggestions won't be appropriate for all businesses, for example you probably wouldn't want to see a therapist in a pub, so pick the ones you think would be appropriate for your business ideas.

8.2 Education and training specific to your industry

Unions and trade organisations (see Section 12.2, page **166** for links) often offer free or low-cost courses and educational events such as seminars; some may offer online events as well. This can be a good way of meeting other self-employed people.

8.3 Physical space

Some businesses need private space. Here are some ideas of how you can find a space, depending on your business.

- **See clients in their homes.**
- **Work with clients at their local gym.**
- **Work with clients outside**, e.g. in a park.
- **Convert a camper/RV or similar** into a mobile consulting room, or buy a **converted one.**
- **Apply for grants to get space.** Also research whether it is normal in the industry/sector you are in to include room hire in the fee or if customers would expect to provide space for you to work in.
- **Share a space:** Use websites like Gumtree, etc., to find people wanting to share their studio/consultancy rooms. Someone may have rented a space for a monthly fee, but want to find other people who will pay to use the space when they are not using it, as this helps them pay the rent. It also makes it cheaper for you, as you don't have the financial burden of a whole month's rent for the space, and can just pay for what you need.
- **Rent a chair or desk:** In some industries it is common to rent a desk, or a space within a space. For example, many hairdressers in the UK rent a chair, which means they pay to use a hairdressing chair in a salon, so they do not have to pay the whole rent for a salon. Some salons may also include other things in the hire charge (cost) of a chair, e.g. use of studio products like shampoos, etc. Many artists will rent a desk space within a studio.

  If you decide on this option, it is important to have a formal agreement between you and the person whom you are renting the chair/desk from (see the relevant trade union for your industry's guidance; see Section 12.2, page **166** for trade union links). Also factor in that you may need insurance and licences or permits to do this, depending on the industry you work in.
- **Investigate local business incubators:** Business incubators may be attached to a university or college.

They usually offer low-cost office space for people starting businesses. Sometimes this includes additional support such as phone answering, signing for packages, mentoring or training. Some incubators are just for students attending the institution they are connected to, but other incubators may let you join without being a student of the institution.

- **Local business centres** may have low-cost office space.
- **Unconventional spaces:** You may find that a large cupboard is a preferred option (this might seem a bit strange, but it works for BBC developer Jamie Knight).
- **Swap some of your time for use of someone else's space:** For example, if massages are what your business provides, offer free massages for a number of hours a month in exchange for using a room for a number of hours.
- **Co-working spaces** may have bookable rooms as well as hot-desking facilities.

 Hot desking: In a space with a number of desks, anyone using the space can use whichever desk is not in use. Desks do not belong to an individual, so you can't store your belongings in or on the desk when you're not using it. You won't always use the same desk (as someone else may be using the desk you like when you arrive at the co-working space).

- **Self-storage companies** such as Access Self Storage in the UK sometimes also rent out office space.
- **Member clubs, sport clubs, community centres, church halls, pubs and hotels** often have bookable rooms.
- **Special offers:** Another opportunity that you may see in a Facebook group is special offers on renting a space, e.g. half-price Wednesday. Finding these opportunities

and being able to think about how they apply to your situation might seem difficult, but a bit of searching on the internet and social media platforms will usually help you find such groups and organisations.

8.4 Using groups to find information

You can use groups to find information and for skill swaps.

 Skill swap: When two people with different skills do a task for each other.

EXAMPLE

A common issue for many musicians and bands who are at the start of their careers is getting their music recorded to a high standard. The cost of this is often unobtainable, but if you are a member of Facebook groups and other information-sharing places you may see opportunities. For example, students at universities and colleges studying music production may ask for bands/musicians to volunteer to be recorded for their projects. This is a great opportunity for many musicians, and whilst it may not be as professional as a commercial studio, it is still good enough so you can send the recording to venues and radio stations, and share it online. You could also contact universities or other education institutions volunteering yourself to be recorded.

 'Hi! I was just wondering if your music production courses need bands/musicians to volunteer to be recorded?'

On the next page, make a list of resources you have easily available to you.

Examples

- Someone you trust willing to do your bookkeeping
- Internet access
- A printer
- A scanner

LIST OF RESOURCES YOU HAVE EASILY AVAILABLE TO YOU

. . . .

. . . .

. . . .

. . . .

. . . .

. . . .

. . . .

. . . .

. . . .

. . . .

. . . .

. . . .

8.5 Planning ahead

If you have equipment you will need to use for your business, such as a laptop or car, you need to make a plan for how much money you will need for this, and how you will save money for maintenance of the equipment or new equipment and insurance.

EQUIPMENT YOU WILL BE USING TO RUN YOUR BUSINESS

....

....

....

....

....

....

....

....

....

....

....

....

8.6 What is investment?

You may hear people talking about growing a business, and investments. These words can be confusing. Obviously, money itself doesn't grow, but the amount of money a business has can increase (sometimes described as growing). Here is a cartoon strip to illustrate the concept of investment.

Jim   Jim's dad

Jim's dad lends Jim £10

Jim spends the £10 buying art supplies

Jim makes 20 greetings cards with his art supplies

Jim sells each of his greetings cards for £1 each

Jim now has £20

Jim pays his dad back the £10 he lent to Jim

Jim uses his other £10 to buy art materials

Jim makes 20 more greetings cards and sells them for £1 each

Jim has £20

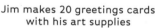

He could keep £10 as profit and invest the other £10 in buying more art materials

Jim has grown his business from £0 to £20

8.7 Where can you get funding or investment for your business?

Many businesses start with no funding. Here are some sources of funding that you may want to investigate to help you start your business.

Loans

If you take out a loan, as well as paying the loan back, you also have to pay interest. This is usually a percentage each month.

> ### EXAMPLE
>
> If your loan was £100 and the interest rate was 2% per month, each month you would be incurring £2 extra in cost. Over ten months, this would be an extra £20 to pay back. Whilst this may not seem like a lot, I have kept the numbers small to try and make the maths easier – what if it was 12% a month?

The interest rate might be per month, three months, a year or some other time period, so you need to check.

Start-up funding

Organisations supporting people to start their business (see Section 3.5, page 53) sometimes provide funding in the form of grants and loans. Where possible, avoid loans as you won't know if you will be able to pay them back.

 Grant: Money you do not have to pay back.

 Loan: Money you do have to pay back.

Government funding

Government funding may be available at a whole-country (federal) level, or state/county level. It might be for a business setting up in a particular industry/sector, for example fishing, or available more widely, as any business activity can stimulate the economic growth of an area.

Social enterprise

If you are interested in running a social enterprise (a business that is not focused on profit but on benefiting a community in some way), there may be funding specifically for this kind of business in your country. See Chapter 15 for more information on this topic.

Specific group funding

Not-for-profits or other organisations supporting people from particular ethnic backgrounds or with a disability sometimes have initiatives to help these groups achieve something such as self-employment, and offer grants or other opportunities.

Crowdfunding campaigns

Crowdfunding is when lots of people give small amounts of money towards a financial goal. The goal could be to fund manufacturing a new product or setting up a new music venue, for example. It is called a campaign because there is often a time limit in which the business wants to raise the money. Many successful projects that have been crowdfunded have involved the people who set up the campaign working hard to promote their campaign and encouraging people to back it.

Some websites that provide crowdfunding don't give the business the money raised unless the campaign reaches their financial goal (either the money donated is returned to the backers, or it is not taken from their bank accounts until the goal is reached within a time limit).

Backer: In this context, a backer is someone who is putting money towards a crowdfunding campaign to help a business reach a goal.

Some businesses set up their crowdfunding campaign to allow for people to pay for a product or service now and get it when the funding goal has been reached and the product is made. Sometimes businesses offer 'perks'. A perk is an item such as a T-shirt that a business gives someone giving them money (a backer of their campaign) to say thank you for supporting them.

A successful example of crowdfunding is the fidget cube (www.antsylabs.com/products/fidget-cube).

Look at what businesses in your industry are using crowdfunding for. Websites that do crowdfunding include the following:

Kickstarter	www.kickstarter.com
GoFundMe	www.gofundme.com
Indiegogo	www.indiegogo.com

Venture capitalists

A venture capitalist is someone who gives money to a business in exchange for a share in the business's profit and/or some control in how the business is run.

Angel investor

An angel investor is someone who puts money into a business and in return asks for a share of the business profits. Angel investors typically are willing to fund very small businesses, or businesses that venture capitalists would think too risky.

Industry-specific funding

You may be able to access funding specific to your industry via your trade union and other organisations (federations, chambers of commerce, guilds, etc.). (See Section 12.2, page **166** for links to trade unions.) This could take the form of subsidies from the government, or specific funds like Arts Council England's Grassroots Live Music fund.

Specific event funding

As I write this book there are funding initiatives, created by governments as well as organisations, to help people impacted by the lockdown due to COVID-19. Other events might offer specific funds, such as the Olympics.

Support in kind

Support in kind is when someone gives you support for free. This is usually not cash (money), but it could be things like office space or mentoring. It may also be 'match funding'.

 Match funding is when you have a set amount of money for a project and you are asking for the same amount from a different funder. For example, if I had £5000 to put towards a project and I wanted to ask a funder for matched funding, I would ask them to match my £5000 and give me another £5000. If I was successful, I would then have £10,000 for my project.

Another example of support in kind could be a family member helping you to run your business.

If you are planning on applying for funding or a loan, you may need a business plan: see Section 18.3, page **256**.

8.8 Review

In this chapter we explored how you can start a business with limited resources (which could be time, money or space). We also looked at what you might need to run your business, what an investment is and where a self-employed person may be able to get funding from.

ACTION POINTS

Tick in the box when you have completed each action point.

1. List the resources you need to be able to do your business idea. ☐

2. Make a list of when you would need to replace or service equipment. ☐

9

Understanding Revenue

9.1 What is revenue?

Revenue means money coming into the business.

9.2 What is a revenue stream?

Revenue stream: An activity a business does that generates profit – for example, selling chairs at a market stall could be a revenue stream, as could selling chairs to large corporations

If you like metaphors

Imagine a river that has multiple streams that go into it. Along the river is a well that needs a little bit of water every day. Further down the river there is a craft beer company that needs a lot of water every week.

If one of the streams that go into the river becomes blocked, there will be less water in the river. This may be OK for the well, but it may stop the craft beer company from being able to brew beer. If the stream was blocked for too long this could cause the craft beer company to have to move or close down.

If you do not like metaphors

Money, also known as revenue, comes into your business from multiple products or services. If one of those products or services becomes unavailable, for example if you ran a removal business and your van or a piece of equipment you needed was broken, the revenue slows or stops. Businesses always have bills to pay (running costs), so this will create a problem with cash flow (no money is going into the business, or not enough money is going into the business to pay the bills).

 Cash flow: The flow of money in and out of the business.

So, a revenue stream is a way to get cash. Having multiple revenue streams will help your business to be more stable.

 Cash in this context means money the business can spend (this could be on credit cards, but remember you will have to pay the credit card companies the money back plus any fees you have incurred, e.g. interest).

 Interest in this context means a percentage that is added on to money someone has borrowed, which they will need to pay back.

EXAMPLE

One revenue stream I have is playing gigs (concerts) as a musician. When the COVID-19 pandemic happened I could only do gigs online, so that revenue stream dried up for a while. But I got some more work with an organisation helping them to communicate and work online. If my only revenue stream was offering gigs, I would not have been able to pay my bills.

9.3 How can you start creating different revenue streams?

When you first start your business you may only be offering one product or service, but try to think ahead about what other products and/or services you could offer, and what you would need to be able to offer the new products/services.

Below are three examples of revenue streams.

Jo – Dog walker
- Dog walking
- Dog sitting
- Dog grooming
- Dog training
- Custom dog toys
- Puppy training

Kim – Freelance data processor
- Data entry
- Data mining
- Transcription
- File conversion
- Virtual assistant

M – Ironing services
- Ironing
- Small grocery delivery
- Clothes washing
- Clothes repairs
- Clothes alterations

9.4 Review

In this chapter you learnt that revenue is money coming into the business and that some businesses have multiple revenue streams, which means they offer different types or categories of products or services to different kinds of customers.

ACTION POINTS

Tick in the box when you have completed each action point.

1. (Optional) List the revenue streams of large companies and small businesses locally to you. This may help you to start thinking about revenue streams. Remember that revenue streams are broad categories rather than specific products. ☐

2. List any potential revenue streams for your business. ☐

PART 4

Plan Your Business

Estimated time to read Part 4: 1 hour 10 minutes

Aims: In Part 4 you will create a clear plan of what you will do as a self-employed person/business, who your customers might be, how you will find them, and what and how you will communicate to them to turn them from potential customers to paying customers.

If this seems a bit capitalist to you, you don't have to see your business just as something that makes money. Running a business gives you the opportunity to benefit other people, whether it's making them feel good by cutting their hair in a style the customers love, making their workday easier by fixing their computer quickly and efficiently, or caring for their pet while they are on holiday and giving them peace of mind and their pet a lovely holiday.

Yes, some businesses are purely focused on gaining wealth or power, but you don't have to focus on wealth and power if you do not want to, and it won't stop you from being able to earn enough money to be self-sufficient.

10

Finding Your Market

10.1 What is market research?

Market research is a tool you can use to learn about customers (it is not compulsory).

Examples of things you might learn from market research:

- Whether it is possible to make a profit selling your product at a price that customers will pay.
- What your potential customers want from a business like yours, e.g. delivery options, car parking.
- What products/services potential customers use now, and how they learnt about those products/services.
- What their needs are.

10.2 How could you do market research?

Steps of how to do market research

1. Where might potential customers be found?

2. Plan questions – Include demographics

3. Go to places identified in step 1 – Observe/ask people

4. Ask your questions

5. Analyse results

6. Review what you learnt

7. Plan what you will do next

8. Test out your ideas

9. Review what you have learnt

10. Repeat steps 1–9

On the next few pages is an example of how you could do market research. (There are lots of different ways.)

EXAMPLE: HOW TO DO MARKET RESEARCH

Step 1: Investigate where potential customers could be found

Eisha and Lilly want to start a business targeted at parents of children under five years old. First they need to think about where parents of under-fives go, and when they go there (so that Eisha and Lilly can find people to ask about their product/service ideas).

Here is a list of some ideas of where Eisha and Lilly may be able to find some parents during their research.

- Online forums, e.g. Mumsnet
- Online social media groups for parents, e.g. kids' clothes swap
- Websites aimed at parents of young children
- Parenting magazines
- Nurseries
- Playgrounds
- Town centre

Some of these might seem obvious, but it is an example of why it is important to give this question some thought.

If Eisha and Lilly decided that town centres could be somewhere to find parents, but they didn't think about the time of day, they might go to a town centre at 8 p.m. This may not be a great time to find parents of under-fives, as most children under five go to bed before 8 p.m. and wake very early, which means most parents will want to go to bed early. If Eisha and Lilly had not thought carefully about this, they might have concluded that parents of under-fives do not go to the town centre.

The same amount of thought should also be given to where *exactly* you should go. Eisha and Lilly may meet very few parents of under-fives if they went to a part of the town centre area that had a lot of student accommodation, bars and night clubs (not because students don't have children, but students with children may not want to live in rowdy apartment buildings). If Eisha and Lilly choose a place that parents would go, such as a supermarket, and a time of day when they are likely to be out and about, they are more likely to find people who would be willing to answer their market research questions.

Optional activity: See if you can think of some more ideas to add to the list of places Eisha and Lilly could go to do their market research.

Step 2: Plan your method and questions, and include demographics

Eisha and Lilly need to decide on some questions that they want to ask. There are lots of kinds of questions they could ask, such as:

- Is there anything about being a parent you would like more information about?
- What would make your life as a parent easier?
- What products or services do you use to help you and your child? (They could provide examples like baby food, books, TV, magazines, etc.)
- What has been the most helpful product or service you have used with/for your child?

If you had a specific product idea, you might ask questions about it. Suppose Eisha and Lilly do have a specific idea, such as an under-fives postal snack box service (similar to Graze but for under-fives; see www.graze.com). They could ask:

- Is it ever difficult to make snacks for your child?
- Do you ever worry about the nutritional value of the snacks you give your child?

Eisha and Lilly could ask about what potential customers currently do:

- Do you buy prepared snacks for your child?
- Where do you buy them from?
- How much do they cost?
- Why did you choose them?
- How did you first hear about them?
- What would you like to be different about them?
- What would make accessing snacks easier?
- How do you do most of your shopping? (For example, online, in supermarkets, independent shops.)
- How often do you shop for snacks for your child?

You could consider using scales — for example:

- On a scale of 1 5 (1 is not likely and 5 is very likely) how likely would you be to buy this product if it cost £10?

Do you have any ideas what questions you might want to ask? I came up with the above questions by thinking about what the world might be like from the perspective of a parent of a child under five. If you find this kind of thing difficult, it's good to ask for help coming up with questions.

DEMOGRAPHIC QUESTIONS

Demographics is a category of questions which gives you an understanding of that person's background, for example age or income. This is important because if Eisha and Lilly just assumed that the people who were answering their market research questions were parents, they might not be learning from actual parents — they might be asking childminders, aunts or older siblings. Whilst you may feel this does not matter, are those people likely to be making decisions on what a child can and cannot have? Probably not, because most of these people will be doing as the parent says. But also, if you collect information about demographics, you can see if there is a difference between, say, siblings, aunts and parents.

Questions about demographics can be sensitive; some people doing market research might hand the questionnaire and pen to the respondent to avoid feeling awkward asking the questions.

Common demographic questions are about:

- gender
- age (in ranges, e.g. 18–25)
- income (in bands, e.g. < £16,000 per year, £17,000– £35,000) per year
- ethnic origin
- education
- occupation (the job they do).

Do not ask people how much they earn as a direct question, as this may be interpreted as rude or intrusive.

In Eisha and Lilly's example, they may ask if the person knows any children aged under five and what their relationship is to that child, for example parent, sibling or childminder. Don't make assumptions such as: 'They look like a parent so I won't ask that question.'

Always have a 'prefer not to say' option for each demographic question. If someone says they prefer not to say, try to be positive so you don't make them feel bad (it's easy to look disappointed, and this can sometimes lead to the person not wanting to answer your other questions).

What demographic questions do you think would be good to ask for your survey?

Step 3: Go to the places identified in step 1

Eisha and Lilly go to a park and approach people to do a paper-based survey. In addition, they make an online survey using a website/platform like SurveyMonkey or SmartSurvey and post it on social media in groups for parents or local community groups.

Where do you think you will go to do your market research?

Step 4: Ask questions

- Be polite.
- Work with someone else if possible, in case there are problems.
- Check with someone you trust that what you are doing is safe.
- Maintain good personal hygiene.
- If someone says no, do not try to persuade them, but move on to the next person.
- If a store asks you to not stand outside their store, follow their instructions.
- Try to respond to what people say in a positive way. For example, if someone says what age group they are in and you think they haven't aged well, try not to show what you are thinking with your reaction or facial expression – you can always say something like 'OK, on to the next question.'
- Is there anyone you can practise your questions on?

Step 5: Analyse results

Eisha and Lilly use a spreadsheet to put all of the information gathered into one place. What would be the easiest way for you to collate all your information together?

Step 6: Review what you have learnt
Eisha and Lilly look at the data they collected to see if there are any common trends. For example, did most parents whose household income was more than £50,000 a year like the product idea whereas parents of lower household incomes were less interested? Or did people of lower household incomes say they would be interested when they suggested a lower price?

Step 7: Plan what to do next
Eisha and Lilly decide to make the snack boxes and test them out by going back to the park where they went to do their questionnaire, giving out free samples and asking for feedback.

Step 8: Test out ideas and collect more information
Eisha and Lilly get feedback that people like their product but want it to be cheaper.

Step 9: Analyse results and review
They collate all the feedback into a spreadsheet and start looking at ways to make their product cheaper, or explore if there are more affluent areas to try their test product.

Step 10: Repeat steps 1–9
Eisha and Lilly think about where they could find parents with higher incomes.

10.3 Tips for doing market research

You could start your market research by searching on- and offline for products or services similar to the ones you will make, sell or provide. Make a list, mind map or cartoon of where you think your potential customers could be found, both online and offline.

It can feel a bit scary talking to random strangers at first, but I have had success saying things like:

'Excuse me, I am doing a survey about a new business. Would you be willing to spare five minutes to do a survey?'

Or:

'Excuse me, I have a new business idea and have a questionnaire; may I ask you my questions please?'

I have found it really helps if you can tell the person how long approximately your questionnaire/survey will take.

Some people will say no. This is OK. Try not to take it personally. The person might just be in a rush, or busy, or not like talking to strangers.

10.4 Informal market research methods

You may feel more comfortable taking a more informal approach to market research. You could use websites like Facebook and other social media platforms or speak to people you know such as friends or family.

You might not include all your market research questions in a more informal approach, but you could just ask something like:

'I am thinking of selling my paintings for £75 for an A5 original. Does this seem a reasonable price to you?'

Or:

'I was wondering if anyone had any advice about how much I should sell my paintings for?'

10.5 Observation as a tool

Don't forget to watch what people do. For example, if you want to open a cafe, sit in a few cafes locally and watch when the cafe is busiest. Where do the customers go first when they walk in? Is there a particular age group or gender of customers? Does this change depending on the day of the week or time of day? Do not approach people inside someone else's business to do market research unless you have the business owner's permission.

10.6 If you don't want to do market research face to face

If you don't want to do market research face to face but still want to ask a number of questions, here are some suggestions of other ways you could do market research.

- Mail/post a survey with an envelope for the respondent to post it back.
- Put a survey on social media.
- Pay for a virtual assistant to do online research for you.
- A friend or support worker could help you.
- Pay a market research company to do it for you.
- Contact an institution (e.g. a university or college) that offers courses in marketing qualifications and ask if any of the students would like to help you, as they need real-life experience to gain their qualifications.
- Make an online survey and print flyers with a web

address or QR code linking to the survey. You could put the flyers up on local bulletin boards (you may need to ask permission to put your flyers up).

WHERE DO POTENTIAL CUSTOMERS GO TO FIND INFORMATION?

Where do you think your potential customers go to find information about products or services that are similar to yours?

. . . .

. . . .

. . . .

. . . .

. . . .

. . . .

. . . .

. . . .

. . . .

. . . .

. . . .

10.7 People stealing your ideas

At this early stage, try not to worry about people stealing your ideas. When you have a product you can get it trademarked. But also, you can come up with other ideas, and they don't have to be completely different. For example, there are lots of books about being self-employed. It's not a new idea, but people keep writing them and each one is different.

10.8 How you can use market research to advertise your products/services

You can use what you learn in your market research to help you when advertising your product/service. In my experience customers like clear messaging; they don't respond well to adverts saying things like 'This washing powder may be better than your current powder' (or whatever your product service is). Instead marketing materials often have claims like 'preferred by eight out of ten customers', 'better than the leading brand', and so on.

If you want to make some claims about your products then market research can be helpful. You need to be able to prove your claims, because whilst you might think something is a wonderful idea, that doesn't mean other people will value it enough to buy it. And if people don't buy your product or service, your business is not financially viable.

Below is an activity to help you think about how market research can be used in advertising.

 MARKET RESEARCH AND ADVERTISING

Nisha and Jamal are starting a business making cookies. Nisha and Jamal decided to make vegan cookies because they were both vegans, and during their market research they found that 60 out of 100 of the vegans they asked found it hard to find vegan cookies. They also found out by visiting local supermarkets that there was less choice of cookies that were suitable for people who are vegan. They think that (1) their cookies are the best because they are vegan and (2) taste better than their competitors'.

How could they go about proving their two claims?

Write down some ideas and turn to the next page for some suggestions. Hint: Use Google to help you.

. . . .

. . . .

. . . .

. . . .

. . . .

. . . .

. . . .

. . . .

. . . .

. . . .

. . . .

. . . .

Claim 1 – Their cookies are vegan: A web search would hopefully lead them to the Vegan Society. The Vegan Society allows businesses to apply to use their trademark. The trademark is a logo that businesses can put on their products' packaging, or maybe on the products themselves, and their advertising material. This would give Nisha and Jamal's cookies vegan credibility.

  www.vegansociety.com

Claim 2 – Their cookies taste better than their competitors' cookies: Taste is individual to the person doing the tasting. For example, some people hate the taste of Marmite or Vegemite, and other people love it.

Nisha and Jamal could do a taste test.

EXAMPLE OF A TASTE TEST

A large cola company has done a taste test and uses the information they collected in advertising. The company sets up stalls in shopping malls and other places that have lots of people passing through. They asked people to taste two unbranded colas, to see which one they liked best. They then used this information to give credibility in their marketing messages.

If Nisha and Jamal did a taste test and wrote down what people said, they could use this in marketing.

For example, they could say that 80% of people preferred Nisha and Jamal's cookies.

Note that this percentage does not say how many people were asked. They might have asked ten people, with eight people saying they preferred their product, or they might have asked 100 people, with 80 people saying they preferred it.

It is good practice to give details of how you conducted your research (this makes you look more trustworthy). You can do this by specifying how many people you asked in small print at the bottom of your advertising materials, for example.

Obviously, depending on your business values (see page **159**), you may feel this way of presenting the information is dishonest as you're not making it easy to find out how big the sample was (i.e. how many people were asked), so you may decide on another way of presenting the information, for example 'Eight out of ten people said they preferred our brand'.

If your business is more service based, you might use things such as:

- customer testimonials (feedback)
- physical proof, such as a show reel (if you are an actor)
- photos (if you make, repair, design or build things).

10.9 Why do you think customers would choose you instead of a competitor?

Competitor: A business offering similar products or services to the same potential customers as your business.

You may feel that you can't compete with a big company on price or quality. But as a small business you can learn to understand your customers' needs and offer them a personalised service.

How many big companies are difficult to contact? Even if they have a phone number that is easy to find, you may have to be put on hold and wait, and/or deal with an automated menu. If you e-mail a big company, how often do you get an automated e-mail giving you a ticket number or telling you to wait? As a small business you can make sure customers get a quality personalised service.

You should also consider what your USP (unique selling point) is.

 USP: What makes you (your business) different from other businesses offering similar services. This could be your location, your skills, your service quality, etc.

If you do care about what other businesses are doing...
Remember your aims for becoming self-employed. Was it to dominate the market? Or just earn a living? If you're not trying to dominate the market, then you could view competitors as sources of inspiration, or as a motivator to be the best in your local area, or an opportunity to think about what you could offer that your competitors do not.

Do you have to be the best in your industry?
As Sarah Townsend says in her book *Survival Skills for Freelancers*, 'Clients don't want to work with you because you're the best in your field. They want to work with you because they like you, you're reliable and easy to get along with, and you show a genuine interest in their business.'

You are fine as you are and shouldn't feel you have to try to be something you are not. Don't feel you have to look or sound a certain way to be successful – just try your best, listen to your customers and be prepared to turn down jobs if you can't cope with a particular client or situation.

If you don't care what other businesses are doing/offering...
This is an understandable viewpoint – they aren't me, so why should I care? But keep up to date with what other

businesses are doing, even if you don't like or agree with what they are doing. It's important as a business to try and be adaptable (**agile**, in business speak). For example, as the internet developed in the 1990s, people began using file-sharing websites like Napster to share music. The music industry resisted change for a long time and other businesses came along and took market share. Universal, EMI and other record labels could have created or partnered with streaming platforms, but they were set against internet downloads of music and thought the problem would go away.

Another example: You may be able to alter the way people access a service you provide. For example, during the COVID-19 pandemic I was not able to deliver training face to face due to the UK government restrictions. I switched the way I delivered training onto online platforms like Zoom and carried on delivering training. A good book to read on this topic is *Who Moved My Cheese?* by Spencer Johnson.

10.10 Customer profiling

You can use market research to help you build a customer profile. Customer profiles are general, i.e. not individual people – not Mr Dodd who lives on your street.

For example, if you are running an online business something you could include in the customer profile is where customers are in the world. Because if, say, you were selling takeaway meals and you were based in London, Canada, you probably would not want to supply your meals to people in London, UK. If you did, the food would take a long time to get there and be cold and past its best when it did!

Are you appealing to a particular part of the market?
You could try researching who your competitors are and what

they don't offer. For example, if you wanted to start a business fixing computers in a town where there was already a business offering similar services, you would want to think about what that business doesn't already offer. For example, do they directly advertise to people who are on a tight budget or people who are nervous about using computers? You could then use market research to check whether there are people who are nervous about computers in the area you want to start the business.

In the activity on the next few pages there are some prompts to help you think about who your customers might be. You may also want to write several customer profiles. For example, in my work delivering training about autism for professionals, I might write a customer profile for:

- teachers in special education schools
- teachers in mainstream schools
- social workers in adult social care
- social workers working with children
- parent groups, etc.

 ## CUSTOMER PROFILE ACTIVITY

What age will your customers be? Is there a specific age group you are aiming at or not aiming at? For example, will kids buy your product, or retired people?

. . . .

. . . .

. . . .

. . . .

Where will your customers be? For example, only in your country, all over the world, in your town or city?

. . . .

. . . .

. . . .

. . . .

Are your products/services aimed at a particular gender?

. . . .

. . . .

. . . .

. . . .

Will customers have a lot of knowledge or a little knowledge about what they are buying?

. . . .

. . . .

. . . .

. . . .

Will customers be buying for work or non-work interests?

. . . .

. . . .

. . . .

. . . .

Do your customers have specific needs, e.g. disability?

. . . .

. . . .

. . . .

. . . .

Are your customers buying your product or service for themselves or for someone else? For example, will they be parents buying for their child?

. . . .

. . . .

. . . .

. . . .

10.11 Review

In this chapter we looked at what market research is, why people do market research and how you could do it. We also looked at what a customer profile is and why they might be useful.

ACTION POINTS

Tick in the box when you have completed each action point.

1. Decide if you are going to do market research. ☐

2. Conduct market research. ☐

3. Write a customer profile. ☐

11

Deciding on Your Business Identity

11.1 What is a business identity?

A business identity is the way that other people can distinguish your business from other businesses. Business identity is also sometimes described as a brand and can incorporate but is not limited to:

- business name
- business logo
- business mission
- business values.

In this chapter we will look at some of the key elements businesses commonly use in their identity.

Why do you need a business name?

You need a business name for invoices, receipts and your web presence (website, social media and directories).

Try to avoid a business name someone else is using (as this could cause legal issues and confusion). Ways to check if your business name is already in use:

- View the government register of companies in your country. For example, Companies House in the UK has a business name checker.
- Web search, e.g. Google.
- Social media accounts: search with the name you want to use.
- Use domain name registration websites, e.g. GoDaddy or 123 Reg, to find out if anyone has registered a web address with your desired business name. Be sure to check both the .com version of the name and also country-specific versions, e.g. co.uk, .be, .jp, .co, .au.

Good business names

Some people use their name as a business name. This may not be a good choice if your name is long, hard to remember or hard to spell.

I use my name as my business name, because for me as a sole trader (see Section 15.2, page **208**) it is easier, and I started my business using my personal bank account. If I had used a different business name, then people may have tried to write cheques to that name, and I would have been unable to pay them into my bank without upgrading to a business account (which would have cost more money). Things are different now with the rise of online banks like Monza and Starling making business banking more accessible.

A good name can also help with advertising, so if I ran a book shop it would be better to call myself Robyn's Book Shop, or Steward Books, or my full name with what I do after it (as with my publisher, Jessica Kingsley Publishers). Sometimes if your business is working in a small geographical area your surname can work well. For example, local to where I grew up is a bus company called Whincop Coaches, which is named after the owner's surname. Surnames are very common in the business world, for example Walgreens (the pharmacy store) and Ford (as in the cars) are both people's surnames.

Strategies to help you think of a business name

- Write down your first and last (sur-) name and your initials.
- Write down words that describe what you'll do or sell or how you do it.
- Combine words that describe what your business does with your initials and first or last names.

For example, you may come up with Mark's Deliveries, Mark's Flowers, Mark's Eco-friendly Delivery, Mark's Speedy Boxes or Mark Speed.

If you're not sure, ask other people what they think.

Make sure your name is not too similar to that of your competitors or other businesses.

11.2 What is a logo?

A logo is like an icon for your business. Think of computer programs you use regularly: each one has its own distinct icon. The icon can help you get to the program or app you want quickly.

If you use Windows then you are probably familiar with the Microsoft logo. If you're an Apple Mac user, then you probably know the Apple Mac logo. You probably also know the Google logo and McDonald's logo.

Logos can help people recognise your business quickly in a directory or other place where they are used. They are also part of your business identity.

Logos can evoke emotions in your potential customers. This might be hard to imagine. But for some people who have a lot of choice of businesses that they can use, the logo is something that might communicate something that the customer values, for example friendliness or professionalism. Maybe when you look at a logo you feel nothing, but consider if there are things you look at that do evoke emotions. For example, animals often make people say aww, syringes can make people cringe, food can make people feel hungry, and the rainbow unity sign for autism might make you feel part of a community.

You do not have to have a logo, but it may help you if it is included in things like directories of businesses.

How can you design a logo?

Here are some ideas for how you could develop a logo.

- Are there any objects, or symbols, that you feel represent your business? For example, if you were a bookshop this could be a book with a $ sign on it.
- List or create coloured dots/splodges of colours you like.
- Look through fonts on your computer and choose which ones you like and don't like.
- Play with the shapes in Microsoft Word, PowerPoint or other programs/applications. Which shapes do you like best?
- Make sure your logo is not too similar to your competitors, and that you have paid for the font if you need to.
- Ask for feedback from friends and family.
- Make a collage of other companies' logos you like and don't like. Are there any similarities between the ones you like that could be incorporated into your own logo?
- Think about anything that makes you stand out, for example glasses or a hat. Experiment with adding these things onto the name or initials of your business.

Using logo builders

There are some online tools that can help you if you are not particularly artistically skilled. If you feel you can't draw your own logo, where can you get free or low-cost help?

Logo builders

- Wix (wix.com) and other website builders have logo design functions.
- Canva (canva.com) is a graphic design platform with a lot of tools to help you create logos, business cards, etc.

- Or you could pay for someone to design you one. Many graphic designers offer logo designing. To find someone to design a logo for you, some websites you could try are:
    - Fiverr (www.fiverr.com)
    - TaskRabbit (www.taskrabbit.co.uk)
    - Upwork (www.upwork.com)
    - Guru (www.guru.com)
    - CloudPeeps (www.cloudpeeps.com).

Common elements of branding

There are other elements of business identity that are outside the remit of this book. However, there are lots of books, websites, etc. with information on this topic. Things to consider are:

- **Mission:** What is your business's goal? For example, to offer the best local cakes
- **Values:** What is important to you as a business? For example, friendly, honest, trustworthy, knowledgeable, being environmentally friendly.
- **Tag/straplines:** A sentence that says what is important to your business or what you do. For example, 'Autism support from a person, not just a textbook.'
- **Brand:** The elements that give your business an identity that is distinguishable from your competitors.

11.3 What is a business card?

A business card is a small piece of card or plastic with the details of a business, or a person within a business. The size of a business card is usually 3.5 x 2 inches (8.9 x 5.1 cm).

Tips for making business cards:

- Make sure the font is not too small.
- Make sure it is easy to read.
- Do not use copyrighted material without permission.
- Make sure it just has the information someone would need to contact you (your name, company name if applicable, what you do, how to contact you/find out more information). Do not include too much information.
- You could use the side of your business card that does not have your contact details on to show photos of your work, or positive customer feedback.

Companies like Moo (moo.com) can print business cards with different images on each card.

How to get business cards

- Hand draw/write and then print.
- Use Microsoft Word or other software to design cards.
- Use online services like Canva (www.canva.com).
- Print your own with a business card template such as the ones made by Avery (www.avery.co.uk).
- Use a website like Vistaprint (www.vistaprint.co.uk) or use a more customisable website like Moo (moo.com).

11.4 Review

In this chapter you learnt what a business identity is, and the basic elements that make up many businesses' identities, including names and logos and where this information is used.

ACTION POINTS

Tick in the box when you have completed each action point.

1. Create a shortlist of possible business names. Ask family, friends and social media contacts which name they like best. ◯

2. Design a logo either by drawing it by hand or digitally, or using an online tool like Canva. ◯

12

Working Out How Much to Charge

Pricing and asking to get paid is a common area of difficulty for many newly self-employed people. In this chapter we will investigate how you can find out what other businesses charge or what is common in your industry/sector, how you can ask to get paid, and how you communicate from the first time someone contacts you that they need to pay you. We will also investigate when, if ever, you should work for free and how you could go about deciding on what you will and will not do for free.

Always consider how much it costs you to make the product or offer the service. To run a successful business you need to price your products/services so you are making a profit, so don't just say, 'Well that person charges £10 for their product, so I will charge £10' – if it costs you more than £10 to make the product, you need to charge more. Also, if your profit margin (how much profit you make) is too small to sustain your business, then you need to consider if it is viable – maybe you need to source cheaper materials, buy in bulk, diversify what you offer or choose a different product or service to sell.

EXAMPLE: MY EXPERIENCE

Up until 2014, I always felt awkward about charging what I charged (which was towards the bottom end of the market rate – that is to say, many people who were doing the same kind of work charged a lot more than me).

In 2014 I went to a gig and saw a J.J. Cale tribute band; the drummer was amazing. I've seen and heard lots of drummers. This guy had brightly coloured drumsticks and brushes; he was expressive with his playing, his body and his face. He was fun and he really engaged with the audience in a way I had not seen before.

I searched for him on Google. His name was Mark Walker, and he has had drumming gigs like being one of the drummers in the West End production of *The Lion King*. He also runs team-building drumming-related workshops. I felt he'd fit into a project I was doing. I e-mailed him to ask how much he charged. When he told me, he was very apologetic, but I thought what he was asking was a reasonable price. His playing had deeply affected me and motivated me to explore jazz trumpet.

Then I understood that if you can do a good job (and I had feedback sheets at this point spanning over five years, that suggested I must be doing something right), you are valuable and you truly can make a life-changing difference.

That one gig was instrumental in changing the course of my life. I started taking myself seriously and being OK with saying I was good at my job and should be paid the same as others doing similar work.

I understood that what I do could be life-changing for someone, for example a teacher, in the way they understand autism, and this could mean that for the rest of that teacher's career they may be able to better support the autistic kids they teach – just as Mark had made a difference to my life in the space of four hours (the length of a half-day training course).

This new confidence meant that when I needed to cost in someone to help me (Sarah Jane; see Section 20.6, on page **272**) I didn't agonise over it.

The e-mail exchange I had with Mark, when the shoe was on the other foot (i.e. I was going to pay for someone else's services as opposed to being the person being paid for services), gave me a new perspective.

You may feel that what you're doing won't change people's lives, but whatever you do will impact on your customer/client's life, even in a small way. Try not to feel awkward about charging the market rate. Believe in yourself and what you do. Also, remember that you did not choose the market rate, and if you believe the market rate is wrong, you probably won't be able to change it on your own anyway. So, while you figure out how to battle it (perhaps through a trade union), accept it for what it is. (**Robyn**)

 Mark Walker's website: www.mark-walker.co.uk

12.1 What are you charging for?

Charge per service
Hairdressers often charge per service – for example:

- cutting hair
- blow drying hair
- washing hair
- bleaching hair
- colouring hair, etc.

Charge for quantity of time (e.g. per minute, or per hour, half day or full day)
If you are a business offering services, such as an IT company, you could offer an hourly rate and set a minimum amount of hours customers can book you for, and then ask customers to set the maximum time they want to pay you for.

Provide a subscription/membership service
Many businesses now offer subscription services, for example a business offering a monthly recipe box, artists' creation box or access to online content. This would usually require some sort of contract between the business and the customer.

People who are self-employed through YouTube and other similar websites, for example making gaming videos, use a membership model. Traditionally this might have been through an online forum or a members area on the person's website, but there are websites such as Patreon that people can use to set up a monthly payment to you to support your work.

Patreon: www.patreon.com

Commission

As an example of commission, you might run a website selling mini spa breaks at hotels. You don't provide the hotel, but are just the person doing the selling (sometimes called the middle man, though this isn't a reflection on the seller's actual gender). You would get a percentage of each sale, known as a commission. For example, if you sold a mini spa break for £100 and you get 10% commission, your profit would be £10. (This is a simplified example – in real life you would subtract the expenses involved in gaining the commission, such as a part of your internet bill and your time (sometimes called labour).)

12.2 Organisations/sources of information to help you work out what other similar businesses charge

- Industry-specific social media groups (e.g. Facebook and LinkedIn), hashtags, forums or meet-up groups (e.g. www.meetup.com).

Search online for your self-employment activity (e.g. 'musician') + 'rates card' or + 'how much to charge'.

- Industry trade bodies/unions.
- Ask your friends and family.

'Do you think this is a reasonable price?'

Or:

 'How much do you think I should charge and why?'

- Ask clients/customers what their price range or budget is (if providing a service-based business).
- Create a survey online and share on social media, asking people their opinions on pricing.
- Look at what other businesses charge, either by visiting them (if they are a store), looking online at their website, asking for a quote as if you were a potential customer, or by looking at their marketing materials.
- Check freelancer unions (see below).
- Find industry specific trade unions (see the next page).

FREELANCER UNIONS

UK

IPSE (Association of Independent Professionals and the Self-Employed)	www.ipse.co.uk

USA

Freelancers Union	www.freelancersunion.org

CANADA

Canadian Freelance Union	www.canadianfreelanceunion.ca

AUSTRALIA

Freelance Australia	https://freelance.org.au

NEW ZEALAND

E tū	www.etu.nz/join

DIRECTORIES OF INDUSTRY-SPECIFIC UNIONS

UK

GOV.UK Trade unions: The current list and schedule	www.gov.uk/government/publications/public-list-of-active-trade-unions-official-list-and-schedule/trade-unions-the-current-list-and-schedule

USA

Dun and Bradstreet Labor Unions companies in the United States of America	www.dnb.com/business-directory/company-information.labor-unions.us.html?page=1

CANADA

Government of Canada Labour organizations in Canada	www.canada.ca/en/employment-social-development/services/collective-bargaining-data/labour-organizations.html

AUSTRALIA

Australian Council of Trade Unions (ACTU) ACTU National Union Directory	www.actu.org.au/about-the-actu/directory

NEW ZEALAND

| New Zealand Council of Trade Unions | www.union.org.nz |

12.3 Common terminology used in business when talking about pricing

Market rate: The amount people usually charge for a product or service.

Market: People who are willing to buy something. In a different context, 'market' could be referring to, say, a farmers market or financial markets.

Market share: What percentage of people are buying a particular product or service.

EXAMPLE OF MARKET SHARE

At the time of writing this book, Spotify has a large share of the online music streaming market. This means that a lot of people use Spotify compared to other online music streaming services (see www.counterpointresearch.com/global-online-music-streaming-grew-2019).

12.4 Ways of pricing products

Cost plus pricing: This is the cost of making/providing the service plus a percentage, for example 10%.

Consumer-led pricing: What people are willing to pay (you would use market research to work this out).

Competitive pricing: Alter pricing based on researching other companies and pricing similarly to them.

Premium and economy pricing: Offering a product or service with basic features and another which has more features, for example when you buy a plane ticket there are economy tickets for basic seats and premium ticket options where you can sit in a more comfortable cabin which has more leg room, fewer rows of seats, bigger TV screens, etc.

 Print: A copy of an original work, often made digitally by scanning the original artwork.

12.5 Using pricing as a promotional tool (i.e. to increase sales)

Add-on: An add-on approach is when some or all components of a product have their own cost. For example, a burger restaurant might offer a burger for £10, and offer additional cheese, tomatoes and other toppings for £1 per topping.

Upgrade: Often used within computing, upgrading is offering more features or a better product or service for more money.

BOGOF (buy one get one free): If you are selling low-cost items, you could sell two for the price of one and suggest they give the second item to a friend or colleague.

Link: If you are selling online and can see that people often buy one of your products with another product, then you could design your website to suggest buying the products together.

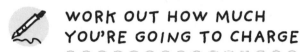

WORK OUT HOW MUCH YOU'RE GOING TO CHARGE

What costs are involved in making and delivering your product/ service?

. . . .

. . . .

. . . .

Will you price per service, per product, or both?

. . . .

. . . .

Which kind of pricing model, e.g. cost-plus pricing, do you think you'll use?

. . . .

. . . .

Will you use any promotional pricing structures, e.g. buy one get one free?

. . . .

. . . .

Where might you look for information about pricing in your industry?

. . . .

. . . .

. . . .

12.6 How do you know if you should do something for free?

Being asked to do things for free, or being offered 'exposure' in exchange for work (providing products/services), is a very common occurrence for self-employed people. Sometimes it is worth it, sometimes it is not.

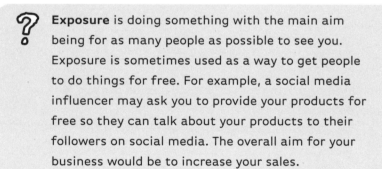

Exposure is doing something with the main aim being for as many people as possible to see you. Exposure is sometimes used as a way to get people to do things for free. For example, a social media influencer may ask you to provide your products for free so they can talk about your products to their followers on social media. The overall aim for your business would be to increase your sales.

(Social) media influencer: Someone who has a large social media following, who lots of people copy. This could be copying their clothing or make-up or a particular action, such as buying a particular brand of clothes or toiletries.

The 'Should I work for free?' tool

Sometimes you might choose to do something for free to gain experience, especially when you are first starting out in self-employment. The 'Should I work for free?' tool below helps you work out if you should do something for free. You can adapt the tool for your own needs.

The tool has questions you can ask yourself; each answer gives a score. The scores can be added up when you have answered all the questions. Practise with the tool to get a 'threshold score' you are comfortable with. My threshold score is 7.5.

> **Threshold score:** The score you need to reach for you to say yes to something you are being asked to do for free.

Create a list of exceptions to the tool. For instance, would you give a member of your family an item of stock without asking them to pay for it? (This probably depends on the cost of your stock, and your relationship with your family.)

Avoid where possible:

- being paid less than the market rate
- being paid less than other people doing the same job
- being paid in gifts, e.g. flowers or chocolates (unless you're happy with this arrangement – oddly, my landlord does not accept chocolate as payment).

Sometimes you may go against your own rules. For example, I have spoken at academic conferences when it has cost me money to do so. Sometimes you make a sacrifice to further your career.

Another possible reason for doing something for free is that it could lead on to doing something that will earn you money. This is a risk as it might not end up earning you money, so you have to make sure you have enough money so that, if the project/piece of work/sale were not to happen, it would not have too big a negative impact on you.

 'SHOULD I WORK FOR FREE?' TOOL

Question	Score
1. If I do this piece of work or give my time for free, will it stop me (either because of time, lack of money or energy) from doing other pieces of paid work? (Yes = 1, Maybe = 0.5, No = 0)	
2. How likely on a scale of 1 (not likely) to 5 (very likely) is it that I will get paying work as a result of working for free?	
3. On a scale of 1 (not at all) to 5 (a lot), will I enjoy it?	
4. Can I use what I do for free in a portfolio or in other ways to help self-promotion? (Yes = 1, Maybe = 0.5, No = 0)	
5. Will it enable me to learn or improve upon a skill, or learn how to do something I didn't know how to do? (Yes = 1, Maybe = 0.5, No = 0)	
6. Will it enable me to connect with more people? (Yes = 1, Maybe = 0.5, No = 0)	
7. Will I be able to swap my time/service/product for something I feel holds equal value? (Yes = 1, Maybe = 0.5, No = 0)	
Total	

Max total 15

Scripts to ask to get paid

 'Is there a fee?' (if you are providing a service to another business)

Or:

 'What is your budget?'

If you don't want the work because the person asking you to do the work won't pay you:

 'Sorry, I do not have capacity right now.'

Or:

 'I'm sorry, I cannot work for free as I have to pay my bills.'

Sometimes people may try to emotionally manipulate you by saying things like 'Oh, but we are a not-for-profit on a limited budget' or 'We are a family on a tight budget', but you have to try to not get emotionally involved in their circumstances. I learnt early on that if you do something for free for one person, other people will also expect you to work for free.

If you feel uncomfortable saying face to face or over the phone how much you charge, you could offer to send the person an e-mail with your pricing structure, or if you were replying to an e-mail you could say something like...

 'Thank you for thinking of me. My pricing structure is attached.'

Or:

'I usually charge [£ amount] for this kind of work. Is that in your budget?'

 Pricing structure: This is a way to explain how your prices increase or decrease depending on the work, the features of the product you provide, or the type of client.

If you are e-mailing to seek self-employed work or sell products, make sure you either include pricing information or say something like:

 'If you would be interested, please contact me for pricing information.'

12.7 Ways to help you feel more confident

Some autistic people providing services such as web design have found it useful to charge less than what other people are charging for the same job, as they feel this is less pressure. It is OK if you want to do this, but think carefully about it, because you risk making it harder for competitors who have larger monetary commitments, and you could anger other people. (This obviously depends on the sector/industry you work in and how bespoke/tailored to the customer your product/service is.)

If you feel worried about your abilities you might consider using the following strategies.

- **Customer guarantee:** 'If you (the customer) are not completely satisfied I (the business) will give you your money back.'

- **No fix no fee:** 'If I (the business) cannot fix your computer (or whatever it is your business fixes) then there's no charge.'
- **Offer a consultation:** You could offer a fixed-rate (always the same cost) or free consultation (set a time limit, e.g. 15 minutes) so you can assess whether you can or want to do the job.

What if you don't want the piece of work?

For whatever reason you don't want the work, for example the customer makes you feel uncomfortable or you are too busy, you can say...

 'Sorry, I do not have capacity right now.'

This is a polite way of saying that you're busy, or simply saying no

12.8 Review

In this chapter we explored how you can seek out industry-specific information for how much to charge for your products/services, some common ways people price products/services, and some ways of pricing that can help with promotions. We also looked at the 'Should I work for free?' tool and developed strategies for asking to get paid.

ACTION POINTS

Tick in the box when you have completed each action point.

1. Research how much other people doing similar things to your business charge. ☐

2. Work out what you are charging for. ☐

3. Plan how much you will charge. ☐

4. Review the 'Should I work for free?' tool: do you need to adapt it in any way for your business? ☐

PART 5

Finding Your Customers

Estimated time to read Part 5: 50 minutes

Aims: In Part 5 we will look at how you can find customers, and how someone goes from being a potential customer to a customer (known as 'conversion').

13

Marketing Your Business

Estimated time to read this chapter: 30 minutes

Before people become your customers, you need to find a way of engaging them and showing them what your business has to offer them. The way most businesses do this is through marketing.

13.1 What is marketing?

The American Marketing Association definition of marketing is: 'Marketing is the activity, set of institutions, and processes for creating, communicating, delivering, and exchanging offerings that have value for customers, clients, partners, and society at large' (www.ama.org/the-definition-of-marketing-what-is-marketing).

 Offerings could be products or services.

So perhaps an obvious next question is: What platform (place) will you use to do marketing? The platform will affect what is possible. For example, you can't include a video in a print copy of a newspaper (well, you could supply a DVD, but it would be expensive – most businesses instead pay for printed adverts).

13.2 Marketing platforms

- Social media
- Your website
- Other people's websites, e.g. guest blog posts
- Industry-specific directories
- General directories, e.g. phone book
- Newspaper and magazine adverts
- Adverts on TV and YouTube, streaming and radio adverts

- Web adverts
- Bulletin boards
- Leaflets/flyers
- Shop front, stall or truck, stalls at expos/conferences
- Signs
- Word of mouth
- Working with social media influencers
- Freebies, e.g. branded pens.

What kind of message do you want to give to attract potential customers?

In the *Guerrilla Music Marketing Handbook* by Bob Baker, Bob suggests that just shouting about your product does not give people anything to engage with. Bob talks about using social media marketing to have a conversation and engage people.

Rather than using social media to shout about your product, aim to engage people. This means that, rather than a person just looking at your social media page/website, they do something with it — for example, writing a post about your content, sharing a post, reacting with thumbs-up, happy or love emojis, or commenting on the post. Engagement is going to mean that potential customers stay on your social media profile/web page (wherever the content is) for longer than if you were just posting adverts.

EXAMPLE OF ENGAGING AND NOT SHOUTING: ALIS ROWE OF THE CURLY HAIR PROJECT

Every Friday morning at 9 a.m. Alis posts her Friday morning conundrum, basically a scenario for people to talk about/engage with. She also posts links to other content, some of which people need to subscribe to her website to access. She is building people's trust that her content is useful, via the Friday conundrum and the posts with content that anyone can access.

13.3 How to get an online presence

'Online presence' is the term used to describe how others see you online. This could be via:

- your own website
- directories
- other people's websites
- blogs
- event listings
- social media.

Common terminology for websites that you might find helpful:

 Website host: A website host is a server (large computer) where many websites are stored.

Examples of website hosts are:

- GoDaddy (godaddy.com)
- 1&1 Ionos (www.ionos.com).

To get a website started you need hosting (meaning you need to pay for your website to be on a server). It's also good to get a domain name, because it will help customers reach you (if the address is easy to remember).

 Domain names are made up of two parts: the address and the domain.

For example, my web address is www.robynsteward.com. The domain part is '.com'.

Examples of domains are:

- .com: Worldwide.
- co.uk, co.au, etc.: Specific to the country the person is in or the business operates in, for example .jp is used by Japan.
- .biz and .info: These can be used by anyone.
- Some domains, such as .gov or .govt, are for special purposes. For example, .gov and .govt are used by governments, and .org is usually used by not-for-profits (charities).

How to get a website

You have a few choices for how to get a website:

- **Website builder website:** For example, Squarespace (www.squarespace.com), Wix (www.wix.com).
- **WordPress:** This is a blogging platform, but many people use it for non-blogging websites. WordPress has less centralised support.
- **Do it yourself** using Hypertext Markup Language (HTML) and Cascading Style Sheet (CSS). You could also use a content management system (CMS) like Perch (https://grabaperch.com) and Joomla (www.joomla.org).
- **A platform** such as Etsy or Shopify.
- **A social media platform** such as Facebook. However, I'd advise against this being your only online presence, because the platform you use, e.g. Facebook, is not entirely in your control. Myspace used to be a very common way for musicians to promote themselves, but is not used so much any more.
- **A profile on a bulletin jobs board** such as Upwork, Guru or CloudPeeps.

How will people find you?

You could use market research to find out how your potential customers learn about other businesses. It's all very well having a nice website or social media page, but it's only good if people are going to it and can navigate around it easily and get what they want from it. For example, if I were visiting a printer manufacturer's web page, I'd probably not be looking for sales information on a printer as I would probably buy it from a store like ao.com, Best Buy or Target, but I might want drivers and manuals. So before you start building an online presence, think about what you want it to do, how people will find you and what they want from your business.

13.4 Scheduling for social media

Many people choose to write social media content (sometimes referred to as posts) in advance of them being published; they use an automated schedule tool to publish the posts at a time of their choosing. Services like Hoot Suite (hootsuite.com) are often used to do this task. For example, you could post information about products on Tuesdays, and funny cat videos on Thursdays.

The point of these posts is not always to sell your products, but to post about things that interest your audience. They are then more likely to follow you on social media, and this means they will be more likely to see the posts you make about products.

 Audience: People who are viewing your social media content.

Funny or interesting posts rather than what are purely sales messages are more likely to be shared. I mentioned funny cat videos as this is something that lots of people like – it has a wide appeal and thus is more likely to be shared. For example, if you shared a video of a cat on the back of a motorbike, this content doesn't require people to have an interest in motorbikes to like and share it. It might then reach the news feed of someone who likes both cat videos and motorbikes, who then clicks on your profile, goes to your web page and buys a product. You also do not have to make all the content you share, for example you can tweet links to YouTube videos, retweet what other people have tweeted and share Instagram posts.

It takes time to build an online following
It can take a long time to get lots of followers who are engaged on social media, but it's important to be consistent. Don't give up just because it's slow. Try your current plan for a month or two and if your followers have not increased in number, think about altering your plan but carry on posting.

Also, it is better to have a small number of followers who engage in high-quality interaction than a lot of followers who do not engage with your content.

13.5 Planning your content

First, think about the reasons people go to the place you are using to market your business. For example, if they go to a bulletin board they are probably busy and need to find the information they want quickly. Or if they are scrolling through Facebook, they are probably having leisure time and don't want sales messages particularly.

If you are passionate or interested in something, for

example motorbikes, and your business has some connection to it, see if you can include that in your marketing. For example, if you sell motorbike-related T-shirts you could share on social media not just the designs of T-shirts but also articles and videos you have enjoyed watching/reading on the topic of motorbikes.

Follow other people on social media who have an interest in or connection to your interests. For example, as well as motorbikes, you might also be interested in related topics such as motocross, Formula 1 racing, the Isle of Man TT race, and so on. Follow people on social media with similar interests and comment on their posts/tweets, etc., not with advertising for your products, but just enjoying having a conversation about topics that interest you. Every time you post, this increases how many people see your name and increases the likelihood of them clicking to view your profile, then going to your website and seeing your products.

You do not have to use all the social media platforms out there. Choose one or two platforms that work for your communication style. For example, if you're more of a visual thinker, Instagram may be a better fit than Twitter, which is less visual.

'I see others less qualified and with less work history and results than me with fancy websites. They seem a bit dishonest as they imply the person is a lot more successful than the reality.' (**Research participant**)

Try not to worry about what other people are doing, but see what you have that they don't (this could be experience or knowledge) as something that gives you an advantage over your competitors. Don't post negative things about other businesses, but rather highlight your strengths in a neutral way.

13.6 Writing a marketing plan

There are lots of books about marketing plans, but essentially a marketing plan is a plan for how customers will find you, what and how you will communicate to them, what you want them to do (call to action), and how you get them to convert (buy something).

 Call to action (CTR): Something designed to prompt someone to buy a product, send you an e-mail, etc.

A tool that may help you to think about your customers' experience and therefore what you can put in place to help get the results you want is a **customer journey**. I will talk about this in Section 14.5 (page **196**).

13.7 Review

In this chapter we explored what marketing is, how businesses advertise to attract customers, and the importance of not just shouting about your products but, on social media particularly, engaging in conversations based around the interests of the business and customers. We also looked at why social media should not be your only platform, and the main options for a web presence.

ACTION POINTS

Tick in the box when you have completed each
action point.

1. Decide what advertising methods you want to try
    first.

2. Decide what platforms will you use for your web
    presence (e.g. social media, website)?

3. If you want to make a website, review the
    different website builders available, try them out
    and choose one you like.

14

Understanding Customers

Estimated time to read this chapter: 20 minutes

14.1 What to do once you and your customers start communicating with each other

I suggest focusing on three main priorities:

- **Impression:** If potential customers get a bad impression of you or your business, not only will they not purchase anything, but they may also tell other people who may have otherwise become your customers.
- **Connection:** If potential customers visit your website or Facebook page, your first priority might be for them to connect with you, and for you to establish a rapport with them and see if your business can benefit them.
- **Conversion:** This is when a protential customer becomes a customer, i.e. they buy a product or service from you.

14.2 How do you make conversions happen?

There are lots of books on how to sell things, but based on my experience when speaking to customers on the phone or face to face, I would take the following steps when trying to sell a product or service.

1. Listen to the customer.

2. Demonstrate that you listened to them using paraphrasing or other active listening tools (see Section 14.3, page **192**).

3. Tell the customer how your product or service will meet their needs. Don't forget that their needs might have an emotional aspect. For example, they may be asking you to paint or decorate their home. Their home is important to them, so they want you to take good care of it. See Simon Sinek's book *Start with Why* and the '5 Whys' (see Section 14.4, page **194**).

4. Ask what their budget is.

5. Tell them what you can offer within their budget, referring back as much as possible to what is important to them.

6. If they say no, that is OK.

7. If they say yes, congratulations!

But what if you're an online business? Then it's about making sure your website, page, newsletters, etc. have a clear 'call to action' (CTA): this is, something you want them to do, such as e-mail you, buy something, share an article on social media, etc. Also remember that even the best salespeople don't get every possible sell.

Regardless of how you are selling, the biggest mistake (apart from rudeness and not listening to or caring about your customer's needs) is to keep using a technique for selling that is continually not working. If your selling techniques are not working for you, analyse what is happening. What are potential customers' responses to you? Instead of buying your products or services, what are they doing instead? Then change something and try again. You might not know what to do, but try something different, then review again and adjust if needed.

If you have in-person business help, or a mentor or mastermind group, ask them for advice. Selling is a skill that you can learn, but as with any skill it takes time.

14.3 How do you tell customers what they want to hear?

When communicating with customers, it can be useful to paraphrase what they have said to you. Use the language the customer has used as much as possible. For example, you may know that the large box that some computers have contains the central processing unit (CPU) and the hard drive, but your potential customer may be confused about these terms. During a sale is probably not the time to correct them – just use their language because that is what makes sense to them. In this example the language misuse is harmless. However, if people are being racist or swearing, for example, you don't have to use their language. I appreciate this may seem like a grey area, which is why it's good to practise with a mentor who can give you feedback.

Also, don't promise what you can't do – it is better to under-promise and do more or do the job quicker than your customer anticipated. However, if there is a deadline set by your customer, make sure to keep to it, and if as the project goes along you find yourself unable to keep to it then be honest.

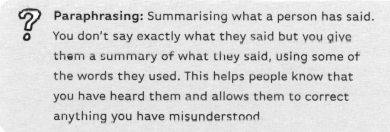

Paraphrasing: Summarising what a person has said. You don't say exactly what they said but you give them a summary of what they said, using some of the words they used. This helps people know that you have heard them and allows them to correct anything you have misunderstood

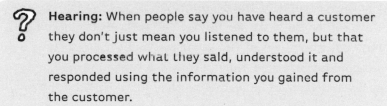

Hearing: When people say you have heard a customer they don't just mean you listened to them, but that you processed what they said, understood it and responded using the information you gained from the customer.

EXAMPLE OF PARAPHRASING AND HEARING

Customer: 'Hello, I wondered if you could help me. I am having a problem with my computer. I keep getting pop-ups and my computer has been slowing down. I think I have a virus but I'm not really sure?'

Computer company: 'Hello, yes, I can help you with your computer. I'm sorry you've been having such a lot of trouble with it. It does sound like you have a virus. I can get rid of that for you, along with the pop-ups.'

14.4 What if customers say no?

Before you start marketing and selling to customers you have to accept that not every person is going to want to use your business, and sometimes people will say no, even if you think using your business would be best for that person. Any person has the right to decline using any business. But remember that when a customer says no, it's not always about you or things in your control.

Why do people say no?
Sometimes the person prefers the business they are using, or they don't like something about what you're offering, for example colour, shape, location or opening times, rather than the actual features of the product.

Also remember that people have all sorts of other things going on in their lives at the point you meet them. Maybe a loved one has just died, maybe they are feeling unwell, maybe they are having a bad day, maybe they just lost their job or maybe they just had an argument on the phone. All of these things can have an impact on a person's emotions.

This may seem obvious now, but when they are in a situation where someone says no and they feel rejected, it is common for people to blame themselves and become too overwhelmed by their emotions to think about it rationally.

Emotions are a big part of what controls a person's decisions. Customers do not have to be your friends; a customer–business relationship is a transactional one. If they become friends that's lovely, but it's not necessary.

5 Whys

Sakichi Toyoda came up with the idea of the 5 Whys. The way this works is you ask yourself a question, and then you answer. Then ask why and answer again, and repeat this till you have asked why five times. For example:

Why (1) is a customer's home important to them?

A: Because they live there and it is a place of safety.

Why (2) is it a place of safety?

A: Because they can go there and nothing bad will happen to them.

Why (3) is that important?

A: Because people can't rest if they do not feel safe.

Why (4) is that important?

A: Because if they rest, they can go out to work and do things they enjoy.

Why (5) is this important?

A: Because it gives the person fulfilment.

Do this exercise for every reason you can think of that a customer might need your product or service, and perhaps every reason that came up in market research too. Review this once a month if you're not selling enough to see if anything has changed (do not ask your customers why five times because it may annoy them). This is a tool to help you think about why your customer buys a product or service (we talked about why they might choose your business instead of your competitors in Section 10.9, page **147**). You don't have to stop at five whys – do as many as you like.

If you get stuck, ask your in-person help, mentor or mastermind group for ideas.

14.5 What is a customer journey?

'Customer journey' does not refer to how your customers get to you, but their experience of your business. Econsultancy, an online website, surveyed 1000 marketing professionals and developed a framework for a customer journey. Customer journeys are outside the remit of this book, but the idea may help you, so do some research about them.

If knowing what your customers might think or feel is hard for you

A lot of autistic people find it difficult to imagine how other people think or feel, or they may think that everyone will think their idea is a good idea.

> **EXAMPLE**
>
> I once asked one of my dad's friends if he had children, and when he said he did, I said, 'They'd love this', and then proceeded to tell him about an imaginary invention for playing with Lego in the back of the car. His children were in their twenties at the time. Not that people in their twenties can't play with Lego, but they would likely be

driving a car rather than being sat in the back, and you can't play with Lego while you're driving! I had to learn that to some extent my opinion doesn't matter. I have to focus on giving my customers/clients what they want.

How do I know what they want? I ask people to fill in feedback questionnaires after a training course. This is a common technique, but with music performances I ask people to write good or bad comments on card stars because giving feedback at a gig is not normal practice. I should also say I am space themed, as my musician name is Robyn Rocket.

Don't underestimate how much you can learn from your customers. When I was teaching older people how to use computers I tried my best to analyse their reactions to things so that I could tailor how I taught them in response to this. For example, if the person I was teaching was struggling to grasp the concept of a menu bar and that you can only see further drop-down menus when you hover the mouse over the menu, I wouldn't focus on trying to get them to use a sub-menu but might focus on things such as finding the help menu and file menu. I wanted them to feel comfortable and not overwhelmed and to be able to learn a useful skill, because that will help to motivate them to keep learning. Whilst I knew more about computers than my customers, I did not know more than them about how they experience using a computer because I have not had the life experiences they have had. Each customer is different, so I was always learning, and for me that was something I enjoyed because I would adapt to each person and I really loved seeing them be able to do something on a computer independently that was meaningful to them, for example whilst I might think that being able to print a document is an important skill, my customers may not be very motivated by that but love seeing images downloaded from an e-mail.

Another tool you can use is an empathy map. This is a tool used by businesses to help them empathise with their customers or potential customers. Follow the link below for more information on how to make an empathy map.

 www.nngroup.com/articles/empathy-mapping

14.6 What is customer retention/loyalty?

Once you have customers it's important to try and keep them your customers rather than them going on to use a competitor. Happy customers will tell other people about your business, but if a customer is unhappy with your business, they will tell other people about that too.

Loyalty schemes

Many coffee shops offer a stamp book. Each time a customer buys a coffee they get a stamp, and when they have ten stamps they can get one free coffee. This kind of scheme could work for anything people buy multiples of, as it encourages them to keep using your business and earning something free rather than going to a competitor (going to a competitor would mean it took longer to get something for free). Also, many people have fixed habits, so once they start going to your business regularly they may well continue to do so.

Discounts

Discounts could be in the form of money-off vouchers given to customers as a paper slip or in an e-mail. This could be an incentive for people to sign up for a newsletter, which means that your customers will think of you every time you send them an e-mail. It could also be seen as a way of rewarding customers, and showing your appreciation for their continuing support of your business.

Responding to customer feedback

In my experience, people like to feel listened to. Asking customers for feedback via online platforms like Google Maps and Trustpilot is good practice, as it will help you learn how to do better, and what you are doing well.

Responding to feedback can also help retention, as customers may feel reassured that if there is a problem with their order/work you have done for them, your business is responsive to feedback and cares about your customers' experience of your products/services. Look at Google Maps and notice how different businesses reply to bad reviews. Some try to help and put the problem right, and others do not. You can also demonstrate you are listening by echoing back and responding to feedback. For example, on your website or a bulletin board you might say, 'You (the customers) said this…' 'In response, we are doing…' As an example, a cake business might get feedback that customers would like vegan options. So they could say, 'You said you'd like vegan options, so we now have vegan brownies.'

Caring about the service/quality you provide

Customer service is really important for small businesses. Remembering customers' names, saying hello to them when you see them and using active listening skills like paraphrasing (see Section 14.3, page **192**) are all ways to make customers feel cared about. The level at which customers expect this will vary business to business. For example, if you were running a day care for kids business, then customers would appreciate any efforts you make to show you care about their individual child, whereas if you ran a grocery store, customers may not want you to know so much information about them.

EXAMPLE OF BEING FRIENDLY AND APPROACHABLE

When I first started my working life, I was working in IT retail. I worked at computer fairs, which are like book fairs but for computers and related products. I noticed that some businesses tried hard to look friendly and talk to customers in a way that they could understand, and not make the customers feel stupid or a nuisance.

Presentation

Some of the stalls at the computer fairs were nicely laid out, with distinct categories, for example displaying all the computer mice, keyboards, etc. together. At other stalls it was harder for potential customers to find what they were looking for.

Some of the people working at the computer fairs paid more attention to their own presentation and appearance than others. Some had branded T-shirts so you could tell which stall they belonged to (which in some cases was also in the business colour scheme), some wore smart shirts, some used deodorants to control how they smelt to others, whilst others were less concerned about how they looked or smelt. If customers associate your business with being professional (e.g. clean and tidy, polite, punctual and getting the job done well), they are more likely to continue using you.

Constantly improving

It is important to not just think, 'I have customers, I have positive feedback, so I will just keep this going.' Yes, keep going, but keep learning about the latest developments in your industry and keep trying to think of ways of implementing customer feedback.

MARKETING PLAN

What do other businesses offering similar products or services do to retain customers?

. . . .

. . . .

. . . .

. . . .

What do you think might be good customer retention strategies for your business?

. . . .

. . . .

. . . .

What is your goal for customers?

Examples

- Buy a product or service once
- Buy a product or service more than once
- Subscribe
- Visit your website

. . . .

. . . .

. . . .

How do you want customers to reach your goal?

Examples
- Visit your website
- Refer a friend
- Call you
- E-mail you

. . . .

. . . .

. . . .

. . . .

How will your customers learn about your business?

. . . .

. . . .

. . . .

. . . .

What might stop them from converting (buying something from your business)?

. . . .

. . . .

. . . .

What will you do to keep that customer a customer of yours rather than going to a competitor?

. . . .

. . . .

. . . .

. . . .

What opportunities will the customer have to advocate for your business (i.e. tell other people they like your business), e.g. button badge, bumper sticker, leaving feedback on your website or a review website?

. . . .

. . . .

. . . .

. . . .

14.7 Review

In this chapter we investigated what to do once you're able to start communicating with customers and how to respond when customers say no, and we also thought about marketing.

ACTION POINTS

Tick in the box when you have completed each action point.

1. Think about the customer journey for your business.

2. Think of the places where a potential customer might come into contact with your business, e.g. on your website, on someone else's website, a social media ad, in your shop.

3. Try to identify your unique selling point (you may have several). Don't worry if you find this difficult; you could consider asking current customers, family or friends for their perspective.

4. What will you do to increase the likelihood of customer loyalty/retention?

PART 6

Formal Business Set-Up

Estimated time to read Part 6: 1 hour 8 minutes

Aims: In Part 6 you will learn what you need to do to set your business up legally, what kinds of documents you will need to make, how to do this and where to find templates.

15

Business Structures and Registration

Estimated time to read this chapter: 20 minutes

15.1 What is a business type and structure?

A business structure is how the tax system sees you, for example whether you and your business are separate entities, and who has control of the business.

First you need to decide if your business is for-profit or not-for-profit.

> **For-profit:** Focused on making profit (see the section 'Common business words' in the Introduction, page **14** for more information about what profit is).

> **Not-for-profit:** Charities/not-for-profits pay staff and people running them, but they are focused on a mission to benefit something, such as wildlife conservation, as opposed to just being focused on making a profit.

Another type of business is a social enterprise. This term means different things in different countries, however, and is outside the remit of this book.

In the UK you can be a community interest company (CIC), which is a type of social enterprise. This is also outside the remit of this book, but see Section 3.5, page **53** for links to organisations that can help.

> **Entity:** Throughout these descriptions you will read the word 'entity' in the context of business structures. This book is a basic book, so for now a helpful way of thinking about an 'entity' is something that can be sold to someone else. For example, I am a sole trader, and if and when I retire,

> I cannot sell my business to anyone else, because nobody else is me. The business and I are not separate entities. I am responsible for any tax or business-related expenses; there is no one else who is responsible.

15.2 What options are there for business structures?

There are different types of business structures. You should seek advice from an accountant or self-employed/business support service when deciding on your structure. You can change business structure in the future if you want or need to. Three options for business structures are:

- sole trader/sole proprietor
- partnership
- limited liability company.

Sole trader/sole proprietor

If you are a sole trader or sole proprietor and your business gets into debt, for example if you bought things for your business on a credit card and had not kept up with your credit card payments, the creditor could take away anything you own, including your personal belongings like your TV.

In contrast, if you are a limited liability company (LLC or LTD), the creditors (the people who lent you money, in this example the credit card company) can't take away things you personally own that are not to do with your business, as it is the business that owes the money, not you. Being an LTD or LLC makes the business and you separate entities; your business is almost treated as if it were a person.

COUNTRY-SPECIFIC INFORMATION

UK

To be a sole trader you need to register for a unique taxpayer reference (UTR). If you already fill out a self-assessment tax form, you may already have a UTR. If not, you can get one from HMRC.

> **HMRC** is the abbreviation for Her Majesty's Revenue and Customs.

USA

In the USA, the term used is 'sole proprietor'. You don't normally have to have an employer's identification number (EIN) (though you may want one), and can use your individual tax number (ITN) instead. You have to make sure you fill in the correct tax form. You can get more information from the IRS (Internal Revenue Service).

CANADA

To be a sole proprietor, you need a business number. You can get this from the Canada Revenue Agency (CRA).

AUSTRALIA

You need an Australian Business Number (ABN), which you can get from the Business Registration Service at https://register.business.gov.au.

NEW ZEALAND

You can use your tax identification number from the Inland Revenue.

EXAMPLES OF SOLE TRADERS/SOLE PROPRIETORS

- J's Art Stall
- Jeff's Food Truck
- Marc the Chimney Sweep

Partnership

Partners in a business are self-employed. The business is not a separate entity, meaning you can't sell it to someone else, but new partners can be included, and partners can leave the business. You can formalise your agreement with other partners using a partnership agreement.

COUNTRY-SPECIFIC INFORMATION

UK

Each partner has to fill in their own self-assessment tax form (or get an accountant to do it).

USA

Not all partnerships need an EIN (employer's identification number).

CANADA

A 'general partnership' can have two or more owners.

AUSTRALIA

A partnership can have up to 50 partners. You can either be a:

- **General partnership:** This is a way of formally recognising that more than one person is running the business, e.g. mother and son, husband and husband. General partnerships do not need to be registered under the Partnership Act.

Or a:

- **Limited liability partnership:** This has at least one general partner and at least one limited partner. Partners who are limited partners have limited liability (responsibility for business debts).

Or a:

- **Incorporated limited partnership:** This is outside the remit of this book – more information can be found at www.business.gov.au.

NEW ZEALAND

Partners could be people or entities (an entity is an organisation the tax system treats as a business rather than people, like a trust or a limited company). Each partner is personally responsible for the business. This is why using entities such as limited companies as partners can be helpful – it means individual people usually have greater protection if the business gets into problems.

Each partner fills in their individual tax form. An extra form for the partnership is needed for declaring tax each year. The partnership needs an IRD (Inland Revenue Department) number.

EXAMPLES OF PARTNERSHIPS

- Dan and Son Locksmiths
- Jay and Jay
- Good Tooth Partnership

Limited liability company

Limited liability means that your liability (responsibility) for business monies, for example business loans, business property, etc., is limited. That is, you are not usually entirely responsible for it. This works differently in different countries (see below). A limited liability company is seen as a separate entity by the tax system.

 Limited means only a certain amount of something, e.g. a cup has a limited capacity (because if you fill it over its capacity the liquid will run out of the cup), and **liability** means to be legally responsible for something.

COUNTRY-SPECIFIC INFORMATION

UK

Limited companies (LTDs) need to register with Companies House. Limited companies have more formal requirements than sole traders or partnerships. One requirement is to have at least one 'officer' (not a police/army officer). Officers have specific duties they have to do. Officers are not considered as an employee or as self-employed.

If an officer is doing work within the business outside of the officer roles (which are very specific: see Companies Act 2006), they can also be an employee. This may be useful if you are trying to manage benefit entitlement because you can control how much an employee gets paid to adhere to benefit rules.

LTDs have limited liability. This is very important for businesses that have assets. Assets could be property – for example, if you owned several houses and were renting them out, the houses would be called assets if you are responsible for paying the mortgage. If something went wrong, for example the business getting into debt (e.g. if tenants in your properties stopped paying rent, which meant you could not continue mortgage repayments), then you personally have limited liability, meaning that the creditors (the business you got the mortgage from, e.g. a bank) usually cannot take your personal belongings such as money, home or car to pay back the debt.

If you want to become an LTD, you should consult an accountant.

Limited companies are really outside the remit of the book, so the above description is just an idea of what is possible.

USA

Limited liability companies (LLCs) are companies with members. There could just be one member or several members. You need to use an operating agreement to define who is responsible for what, for example doing the bookkeeping, how profits are divided between members, and to demonstrate that your LLC and you are separate entities. Members are still considered self-employed. One of the major advantages of an LLC is the corporate veil.

> **Corporate veil:** This defines what the LLC owns in terms of assets such as stock or buildings (property). If the LLC gets into financial difficulty, creditors (people who have lent the business money) can only take things that belong to the LLC, and not the things that belong to its members, hence the term 'limited liability'.

If you have multiple members in your LLC, you will usually need an EIN (employer's identification number) even if you do not have employees.

CANADA

Corporation is the word used in Canada for a business with limited liability. When people start a corporation, they use a charter (formal document) to agree the responsibilities of the people running the business. It costs more to run a corporation, so people don't usually become incorporated (become a corporation) until their turnover (how much money is coming into the business without deducting expenses) is C$50,000 or more.

There are two kinds of corporations, provincial and federal.

- **Provincial corporation** limited liability is a good option if you will only be serving customers in your province.
- **Federal corporation** limited liability makes it easier to do business activities in different provinces to the one your business is based in.

AUSTRALIA

Company is the word used in Australia for a business with limited liability. Companies need shareholders, which could be the director(s). This could be the same people who are running the business, or it could be different people.

Companies are separate entities within the tax system, and benefit from limited liability. See the Corporations Act 2001 for more information.

NEW ZEALAND

Company is the word used in New Zealand for a business with limited liability. You need to register through Companies Office. You can register for a business IRD (Inland Revenue Department) number and Goods and Sales Tax (GST).

EXAMPLE OF A LIMITED LIABILITY COMPANY

Abi's Scooters
Abi rents/hires out electric scooters.
Electric scooters are expensive, and by
using the LLC (or LTD) business type,

Abi can protect himself, his home and other things he personally owns. For example, if Abi had more bookings to hire scooters than he had scooters, he might decide he would lease (formally borrow and pay for the use of something) some scooters from another company. If he didn't keep up to date with his payments and he was a sole trader/sole proprietor, the company leasing the scooters to Abi could take his personal property, for example TV, house and so on, to pay back the money he owes. Being an LLC or LTD means the company whom Abi owes money to can only take things belonging to the business, not things belonging to Abi personally – therefore you could say that Abi has limited liability.

Note that this is a simplified example; in the UK, before taking someone's possessions the creditor would have to go to court to get a legal document called a writ (also known as a writ of control), which allows debt collection officers/bailiffs to take things to pay back a debt. Being in debt does not allow another business owner to personally come round your house and take things themselves; there is a legal process that must be followed. If this concerns you, use the in-person help resources in Section 3.5 (page **53**) and find out how this process works in your country.

Co-op

> **Co-op:** A business that is owned by its members. Who the members are will depend upon the co-op. Each member has an equal say.

Co-ops can use the same business types as other businesses, but the control of the business may be different, as co-ops are

controlled by their members. The members of a co-op could be employees or other people, depending on the co-op. For example, a housing co-op's members might be tenants of a house. Each member of a co-op has an equal say on decisions about how the co-op is run and how money is managed and spent. Co-ops usually are not focused purely on making a profit, but have other social aims, for example enabling people to afford rent in an expensive city like San Francisco or London, or providing employment for people who value having an equal say in how the business is run.

COUNTRY-SPECIFIC RESOURCES

UK

Community Shares Unit Guidance Materials	https://communityshares.org.uk/about-cooperative-and-community-benefit-societies
Cooperative UK	www.uk.coop

USA

Democracy at Work Institute Information for Start-Ups	https://institute.coop/tools/for-worker-coops/start-ups

CANADA

Government of Canada Information Guide on Co-Operatives	https://www.ic.gc.ca/eic/site/106.nsf/eng/h_00073.html

AUSTRALIA

Business Council of Co-Operatives and Mutuals	https://bccm.coop

NEW ZEALAND

Cooperative Business New Zealand Starting Up a Co-Op	https://nz.coop/ starting-up-a-co-op

In the UK you can also have a community benefit society, but this is outside the remit of this book.

In Australia, there is an additional business type, called a trust.

Trust: A trust deed (formal document) is used to set up a trust. A trust is managed by trustees on behalf of the beneficiaries.

Choosing the right business structure

You can change your business type/structure in the future if you need to. More information on choosing the right structure is given below. If you're not sure which to choose, then seek advice from the organisations listed.

COUNTRY-SPECIFIC RESOURCES

UK

Companies House: Choosing the right business structure	https://companieshouse.blog.gov. uk/2018/07/18/choosing-the-right-business-structure

USA

| US Small Business Administration: Choose a business structure | www.sba.gov/business-guide/launch-your-business/choose-business-structure |

CANADA

| Business Development Bank of Canada (BDC): Choose the right structure for your business | www.bdc.ca/en/articles-tools/start-buy-business/start-business/advantages-different-business-structures |

AUSTRALIA

| Australian Taxation Office: Choosing your business structure | www.ato.gov.au/Business/Starting-your-own-business/Before-you-get-started/Choosing-your-business-structure |

NEW ZEALAND

| Business.govt.nz: Business structure overview | www.business.govt.nz/getting-started/choosing-the-right-business-structure/business-structure-overview |

15.3 How do you register as self-employed?

When you are ready to be formally self-employed you need to register. To do this you need to know what kind of business structure you want to have. A business structure is important because if you're going to earn enough money to pay tax, by law, you have to be in one of the recognised structures. This is because the business type/structure will affect how you will pay tax and also may have some legal implications.

How you register as self-employed will depend on where you live. If you need more help, you can use services such as your local small business centre or growth hub.

 Search online for 'How to register as self-employed in [insert name of your country, state or province]'.

UK

GOV.UK: Working for yourself	www.gov.uk/working-for-yourself

USA

US Small Business Administration: Small business administration	www.sba.gov/business-guide/launch-your-business/register-your-business

CANADA

Government of Canada: Registering your business with the government	www.canada.ca/en/services/business/start/register-with-gov.html
BizPal: Online business permits and licences	https://smallbusiness.alberta.ca/bizpal

AUSTRALIA

Australian Business Register: Applying for an ABN (Australian Business Number)	www.abr.gov.au/business-super-funds-charities/applying-abn
NEIS (New Enterprise Incentive Scheme)	https://employment.gov.au/self-employment-new-business-assistance-neis

NEW ZEALAND

RealMe: Secure way to prove your identity online	www.realme.govt.nz
Business.govt.nz: Guide to starting a business	www.business.govt.nz/getting-started/taking-the-first-steps/10-step-guide-to-starting-a-business
Inland Revenue: IRD numbers for individuals	www.ird.govt.nz/managing-my-tax/ird-numbers/ird-numbers-for-individuals

Licences and permits

Some industries require licences and permits. Licences and permits are either federal (country-wide) administrated or state/locality specific. Your local business development centre, small business administration organisation or in-person help (see page **53**) can guide you as to what would be applicable to your business.

Permits normally allow you to be in a particular place and trade (sell products or services) as a business, for example a busker being allowed to busk in a particular area.

Licences often cover a wider geographical area (e.g. a state or country) and/or specific time period (e.g. 12 months), and allow you to do a particular profession (e.g. to be a hair stylist in the USA). Sometimes products need licences, for example food or drink items in the USA.

Licences are often used to make sure a particular standard (set of rules or guidelines) is kept up. For example, a training organisation might sell licences for other trainers to deliver a training programme that the training company has developed; the purpose of the licence would be to ensure that the training is always high quality, as well as ensuring that the training company who designed the training programme makes some profit from something they have created.

Below are links to national licence and permit information, but there may also be specific licences or permits required for the region you work or live in. For example, some councils in the UK require buskers (musicians who perform on the pavement/sidewalk or in a train station or similar) to have a licence to perform in that council's area of control (jurisdiction).

COUNTRY-SPECIFIC RESOURCES

Make sure you also check with in-person help providers (see Section 3.5, page **53**) whether there are specific licence/permit requirements in your location.

UK

GOV.UK	www.gov.uk/licence-finder

USA

US Small Business Administration	www.sba.gov/business-guide/launch-your-business/apply-licenses-permits

CANADA

BizPal	www.bcbizpal.ca/?b=59

AUSTRALIA

Australian Business Licence and Information Service (ABLIS)	https://ablis.business.gov.au

NEW ZEALAND

Ministry of Justice	www.justice.govt.nz/tribunals/ licences-certificates/secondhand-dealers-pawnbrokers/apply/ apply-for-a-company-licence

Contracts

A contract is a legal agreement between two or more people or organisations. Contracts are useful to make sure customers pay you, as contracts can be used to go to court to get paid if a customer does not pay you.

Good sources for contract templates are trade unions/ societies/associations, either a general self-employment union like the UK's IPSE (Association of Independent Professionals and the Self-Employed), or industry-specific associations such as the UK's Society of Authors (see Section 12.2, page **166** for links to country-specific and industry-specific trade unions).

If you are really stuck you could use an online service like Rocket Lawyer (www.rocketlawyer.com). There are also services that provide templates for specific uses. For example, Termly (https://termly.io) provides terms and conditions templates for websites.

COUNTRY-SPECIFIC RESOURCES

UK

Small Business Commissioner	www.smallbusinesscommissioner. gov.uk/home-page/check-your-contracts

USA

SCORE	www.score.org/blog/how-write-business-contract

CANADA

Government of Ontario	www.ontario.ca/page/contracts-best-practices-and-types
BizPal	https://services.bizpal-perle.ca

AUSTRALIA

Small Business Development Corporation	www.smallbusiness.wa.gov.au/business-advice/legal-essentials/contracts-and-agreements

NEW ZEALAND

Business.govt.nz	www.business.govt.nz/risks-and-operations/dealing-with-customer-complaints/what-you-need-to-tell-customers

Do you need a business bank account?

This depends on what country you live in, and your business structure. You can usually start a business with just your normal bank account if you are using the sole trader/proprietor structure but note my words of caution on this topic (see page **21**).

15.4 Review

In this chapter we covered the main kinds of business structures available to people when they first start running a business, and how you register as self-employed.

ACTION POINTS

Tick in the box when you have completed each action point.

1. Decide on a business structure. ◯

2. Register as self-employed. ◯

3. (Optional) Gather the required legal documents to ◯
   register, e.g. operating agreements.

16

Tax

16.1 What are business and tax years?

DISCLAIMER: I have done my best to incorporate information for all the countries JKP mainly sell to. Please be sure to check with in-person help (see page **53**) to clarify how the rules apply to you and your business.

Businesses have a tax year, which is the period of time used to work out how much tax you owe, and sometimes a separate business year, which is used for bookkeeping (see Chapter 17 for information on bookkeeping).

When you start a business you can choose when your business year starts. Sometimes it makes sense to start at a different time to the tax year. You should ask an accountant for help with this.

Both the tax year and the business year are relevant when doing bookkeeping and filling in tax returns. Your tax return is usually for a specific tax year, for example 2019/2020.

Each country has a tax year.

Country-specific tax years
UK: 6th April–5th April.

USA: You can choose to use the calendar year, i.e. 1st January–31st December, or the fiscal year, which is 1st October–30th September.

Canada: You can choose your own business year.

Australia: 1st July–30th June.

New Zealand: 1st April–31st March.

You should check how your country wants you to provide information.

You can often move your business year to line up with the tax year. You need to do this formally with the government department who deal with tax. Some people find business and tax years being the same makes bookkeeping easier.

16.2 What is bookkeeping?

Bookkeeping refers to listing down all the money you have spent for business purposes, or if your business is a separate entity (LTD, LCC or company), the money the business has spent. Money spent is called **expenditure**. All the money that has been paid or given to you (including grants) that relates to your business is called **income**.

Why is bookkeeping important?

Bookkeeping, whilst not a legal requirement in all countries, is important because this is information that you need to meet your legal obligation to fill in your tax return/self-assessment tax return.

16.3 What is a tax return?

A tax return, or in some countries tax self-assessment, is a form that lets the government know how much money you have spent as a business and how much money you have had coming in, as well as information on deductibles and other allowances. This is the form used to formally record your earnings, and is the form used to work out how much tax you owe if you are a sole trader/proprietor.

You could be audited by the tax service in your country. They will want to see all your receipts, invoices, etc. Each country has a limit of how long you have to keep your receipts (e.g. six years in the UK and three years in the USA). By law, you have to provide this information to them if they ask for it.

Tax returns have deadlines that you must keep. You must lodge (also known as 'file' or 'submit', dependent on what country you're in) your tax return before the deadline, otherwise you may have to pay a fine. Accountants can do this for you, and in some countries, if you have an accountant, you get an extension on the time limit for submitting your tax return.

16.4 What does tax deductible mean?

A business expense is sometimes described as a **deductible**. You might say, 'This hard hat is tax deductible.' Suppose you earned £25,000 in 2019, and you spend £1000 on expenses, i.e. tax deductibles. The tax authority (e.g. HM Revenue and Customs, Canada Revenue Agency, Internal Revenue Service) would work out how much tax you had to pay that year by subtracting £1000 (your expenses) from £25,000 (your income), to give a net profit of £24,000, and work out how much tax you have to pay based on this profit.

 Azaria Bell on YouTube did a great video about this, called Tax Deductions – How Do They Work?: www. youtube.com/watch?v=0Fdb1odYW7E

I strongly advise using an accountant, because as well as tax deductibles there are other rules that can benefit you. For instance, when you write a book in the UK you can spread your profit over two years, which can help even out two years of tax bills. I'd have never known this on my own.

Tax deductibles can include using part of your home for business. This is often worked out as a percentage of the value of your home (e.g. you use 10% of your home for business purposes). You can incorporate part of your bills, like electricity and internet, mobile phone contract and mobile phone, and you can employ your children (consult the relevant laws) – this could be a good way to help a young person learn how to run a business and get paid, without the responsibility of a formal role such as officer or director. You can also include attending conferences and events, including conference fee, flights, hotels and often food and drink (keep a log of the distances travelled as mileage is also deductible).

When you input information into your books (do your bookkeeping), whether that is via a spreadsheet or bookkeeping software like Xero or QuickBooks, you will need to list things in the correct category. Each business is slightly different in what counts as a business expense; for example, I could not claim that a hard hat, safety glasses and an angle grinder are business expenses because I do not do any business activities that require them.

To find tax deductible categories for your country, search 'Tax deductible' + 'country' + 'business structure'.

16.5 What are your tax obligations?

Tax obligations vary between countries (and in some cases states) and business structure, as well as on how much profit you make. The information below is based on someone being a sole trader/proprietor. You should check with the tax office or in-person help (see Section 3.5, page **53**) to clarify your tax obligations.

Country-specific tax obligations

Note that income tax rates and bands, personal allowances, National Insurance rates and so on change regularly. The figures below are what applies at the time of writing, so only take these as an example. Obviously none of this information takes into account individual circumstances.

UK

INCOME TAX

This is a percentage of your profit. Different percentages apply for different profit bands. You don't pay income tax if your earnings are less than £12,500 (your 'personal allowance'), and you only pay income tax on earnings above the personal allowance. For example, if you made a profit of £15,000 in one year, you would only pay tax on £2,500 because you do not pay tax on the first £12,500 of your earnings. You would pay tax at 20%, which would give you a tax bill of £500.

Profit £	0–12,500	12,500–50,000	50,000–150,000	150,000+
%	0	20%	40%	45%

NATIONAL INSURANCE CONTRIBUTIONS

If your profits are above £6475, you'll pay Class 2 National Insurance of £3.05 a week (£158.60 per year). If your profits are between £9500 and £50,000, you will pay Class 4 contributions, which are 9% of your profit.

IMPORTANT! When your tax bill is more than £1000 a year, you will start paying tax bills every six months (this is to try and make the tax bill more manageable). The first year your tax bill is £1000 or more you will be asked to pay your tax bill plus an estimate bill for the next six months.

VALUE-ADDED TAX (VAT)

This is a tax that is added on to most goods. If you are not registered for VAT (and you don't need to be if your turnover is less than £79,000 per annum (year)), then you don't have to register to pay VAT. Some businesses choose to register for VAT before they have to as when they buy goods from other businesses they can claim the VAT back, therefore reducing their costs.

So, you pay:

Income tax +

National Insurance Class 2 if applicable +

National Insurance Class 4 if applicable +

VAT if applicable.

You'll get a tax bill either once a year or, if your annual tax bill is £1000 or more, twice a year.

USA

INCOME TAX
At your own personal level as it would be if you were employed.

STATE INCOME TAX
Some states also charge an additional state income tax.

SELF-EMPLOYMENT TAXES
You may need to pay 15.3% of profits.

SALES TAX
This is dependent on which state you are in.

USE TAX
This is due (you would pay this) if you need to buy something

for your business from a different state to the one your business is registered in.

So you pay:

Income tax +

State income tax +

Self-employment taxes +

Sales tax +

Use tax.

CANADA

INCOME TAX

Income tax is calculated as:

Profit C$	0–48,535	48,535–97,069	97,069–150,473	150,473–214,368	214,368 +
%	15%	20.5%	26%	29%	33%

HARMONISED SALES TAX (HST)

You also have to charge your customers 5% **Goods and Sales Tax (GST)**, and **provincial sales tax**, which you also pay back to the government. These two taxes are collected together and are known as **HST**.

All of this information was obtained at the Government of Canada website, Canada.ca.

So you pay:

Income tax +

HST tax.

AUSTRALIA

INCOME TAX

Like the UK, Australia has profit bands. If your profit is below A$18,200 you pay no tax, but you are taxed on your profit above this amount. If your profit was A$20,000, for example, you would be taxed on A$1,800 at 19% so your tax bill would be A$342.

Profit A$	0– 18,200	18,200– 45,000	45,000– 120,000	120,000– 180,000	180,000 +
%	0	19%	32%	37%	45%
Annual cost			+ A$5092	+ A$29,467	+ A$51,667

GST (GOODS SALE TAX)

You don't have to register for GST until your profit is A$75,000 or over, but some businesses prefer to register for it earlier.

Unlike in some countries, your pension is not included in taxes – you have to opt into superannuation (often referred to as 'super'). You can find more information at Moneysmart: https://moneysmart.gov.au/how-super-works.

So you pay:

Income tax +

GST if you want to register for it.

NEW ZEALAND

INCOME TAX (ALSO KNOWN AS PROVISIONAL TAX)

Income is taxed in bands. For instance, if you earned NZ$15,000, NZ$14,000 would be taxed at 10.5%, and only NZ$1000 (the amount over NZ$14,000) would be taxed at 17.5%.

Profit NZ$	0– 14,000	14,000– 48,000	48,000– 70,000	70,000 +
%	10.5%	17.5%	30%	33%

ACCIDENT COMPENSATION (ACC) LEVIES

This funds claims for injuries to you or people working with you. You can find out more information about this at the Accident Compensation Corporation website: www.acc.co.nz.

GST (GOODS AND SERVICES TAX)

If your profits are NZ$60,000 or more per year you will need to register for GST. You add it to the price of your goods, and pay it back via your tax return, but you'll also be able to get GST back on things you have bought as part of your business activities.

So you pay:

Income tax +

ACC +

GST if applicable.

16.6 Do you need a pension?

Being self-employed also means being responsible for your pension. Most governments have pension schemes, sometimes described as a 'state pension', but you may also want to pay into a private pension. This is the equivalent of a company pension, which may be offered to you if you worked for a company or institution. Many employers offer employees the opportunity to pay a percentage of their salary into a pension scheme. If you are self-employed you might not have the money to set up regular payments when you start your business, but you should still have a plan of when you want to review starting a pension.

PAYE

In the UK, you can do self-employed work alongside contracts of employment (i.e. PAYE – Pay As You Earn). Make sure you know if a contract or piece of work being offered to you is PAYE or self-employed, as you need to declare employed and self-employed income in different places on the self-assessment tax form. Seek guidance from an accountant if you need more clarification.

Personally, I prefer that I am not employed, and instead look after my own tax. I find this more manageable. But plenty of people have a mix of self-employed and employed income.

It's important to clarify which type of work a contract is for, and to fill in the right bit of a tax return, so you don't under- or overpay tax. In the UK, HMRC have rules called IR35 about when you are and are not self-employed.

If this is an issue of concern for you, an accountant can help. If you can't afford to pay an accountant all the time, you might consider asking for a one-off advice session with the accountant (they might offer this for free/pro bono).

> **Pro bono** is a word used to describe someone working for free.

16.7 Review

In this chapter we explored what business and tax years are, what your tax obligations are, how tax is worked out, what tax deductibles are, and how to find details for your country.

ACTION POINTS

Tick in the box when you have completed each action point.

1. Know when your business and tax years will start and finish. ☐

2. Research tax deductibles in your country and with your business structure. ☐

3. Familiarise yourself with the tax requirements for your country and business structure. ☐

4. Find an accountant and get a quote for them to do your tax return. (See page **242** for reputable sources of accountants.) ☐

17

Bookkeeping

17.1 How can you do bookkeeping?

You can do bookkeeping in the following ways:

- on paper
- on a spreadsheet
- on a software package.

On paper or in a spreadsheet

I have grouped these methods together as they use similar procedures. You can do bookkeeping by hand either on ordinary paper or in an accounting ledger book that you can buy, which has all the columns you need marked out for you.

Spreadsheets are very much like a ledger book, except they are more customisable and do the maths for you.

Software packages

Software packages for bookkeeping come in two main categories, cloud-based and local software.

In **cloud-based packages**, the information is stored in a server (a large computer that serves information to other computers) on the internet, so you can access your information on your phone or other devices while away from your computer. Popular cloud bookkeeping software packages include Sage, QuickBooks, Clear Books and Xero. Most offer a free trial and I'd recommend you try a few. Some, such as Xero, allow you to invent a fictitious company for the purposes of practising using their system in a safe environment.

Usually you have to pay a monthly subscription for cloud-based software, but this can be inexpensive. Some bookkeeping software allows you to integrate your bank account so your bank statement appears in the bookkeeping software, and you can 'reconcile' it (this means to match the payments out with the appropriate tax deductible categories and the money paid into your bank account with the invoices they correspond to; see Section 16.4, page **228** for more information on this). Some, likes Xero in New Zealand, allow you to fill in your tax return within the software.

Information in **local software** packages isn't stored online, but just on your computer or the device you use the software on.

How do you manage receipts?

If you are good at keeping small bits of paper neat and organised, this is a great skill for a self-employed person. But if you're like me and tend to be somewhat disorganised in nature, you can now get software/apps (sometimes this functionality is built into the bookkeeping software), such as Xero or Dext, where you can take a photo of your receipt and it will digitise the details for you and put it into a spreadsheet, or you can look through it on an app.

Also note that you need the itemised receipt, not just the credit/debit card receipt.

How often do you need to do your books (bookkeeping) and tax return?

You do your bookkeeping as often as you want – daily if you like. Other common frequencies are once a month or once a quarter.

 Quarter: In this context, a quarter is a three-month period, which divides the year into four parts, or 'quarters'. January–March is one quarter, April–June is another quarter, July-September is another, and October–December is another. Note that this is just an example, and your business year or tax year may be divided differently to this example.

Tax returns generally happen once a tax year, but you may pay tax more than once a year.

What happens as my business grows?
Sometimes the rules change when you start earning a lot more money. Business centres or similar organisations could advise you on this (see Section 3.5, page **53** for in-person help).

17.2 What is a bookkeeper?

You can pay someone to do your bookkeeping for you, or a family member or friend may be willing to do it. But it must be someone who you completely trust, and if you pay someone you can control how it is done. For example, my mum did my bookkeeping for the first nine years of my business. I wanted to make my invoicing and managing receipts easier (because I was bad at it) and my mum was not keen on this idea. This caused an argument which I wish I hadn't had to have. My mum agrees that using digital assistance from Xero and Dext has made the bookkeeping easier and now I can do it independently.

17.3 What is an accountant and when should you use one?

An accountant is someone who can prepare the legal record of the money you have had come into the business (income) and money you have spent on behalf of the business (expenses). In the UK an accountant can legally fill in your tax return on your behalf. They will have knowledge of all the relevant deductibles that are applicable to you as well as any allowances that may work in your favour.

Having the formal reports that an accountant can produce is not a legal requirement if you are a sole proprietor/trader. Other business structures (see Chapter 15 for information on business structures) require specific reports which are best written by an accountant.

Using an accountant will help you give the benefit/welfare systems the information they need so they can treat you fairly (the people who work within the benefit/welfare system will probably have not had experience in self-employment).

An accountant can also help you pay less tax, because accountants are trained to understand the tax system and what the rules are for your business and sector.

The reports an accountant can produce may also be helpful for obtaining funding (see Section 8.7, page **121** for information about funding sources).

Always check that your accountant is legally qualified to do the work you are asking them to do.

What if I am unable to afford an accountant?
If you can't afford an accountant, there might be a possibility of skill exchange. Try putting up a post on a social media site or asking friends you trust for recommendations of accountants, contact them, explain your situation and offer a skill exchange. For example, if you're a dog walker how many hours would your accounting needs cost in dog-walking hours? If you usually charge £10 an hour and accountancy costs £200, that's 20 hours, so basically a once-a-week walk with your accountant's dog for four months. If they live local to you and you're just starting out and don't have too many clients, this arrangement may be feasible for you both.

But remember that accountants have to pay their rent/ mortgage and bills too, so they may not be in a position to offer a skills swap.

REPUTABLE SOURCES OF ACCOUNTANTS

UK

Qualified accountants are known as chartered accountants

Institute of Chartered Accountants England and Wales (ICAEW)	www.icaew.com
Institute of Chartered Accountants Scotland (ICAS)	www.icas.com
Chartered Accountants Ireland	www.charteredaccountants.ie

USA

Qualified accountants are known as certified public accountants (CPA)

American Institute of Certified Public Accountants (AICPA)	www.aicpa.org
Association of Chartered Certified Accountants	www.accaglobal.com/hk/en/about-us.html

CANADA

Qualified accountants are known as chartered accountant professionals (Canadian CPA)

Canadian Institute of Chartered Accountants (CICA)	www.cpacanada.ca

AUSTRALIA AND NEW ZEALAND

Qualified accountants are known as certified practising accountants (CPA)

There are also chartered accountants. You can find them at Chartered Accountants Australia and New Zealand (CA ANZ)	www.charteredaccountantsanz.com

17.4 Example bookkeeping

Expenses: Money out

Date	Supplier	Payment method	Amount (spent)	Description	Travel	Consumables
14/09/20	Office depot	Credit card	£2.10	Stamps		£2.10
14/09/20	UK Rail	Debit card	£10.90	Train ticket to training event	£10.90	
Totals			£13		£10.90	£2.10

Notice that each expense is listed twice, once in its category, and once in the amount column. This is so you can add up the full amount spent in each category. For example, you can work out how much you spent on travel.

The categories refer to tax deductibles. I have only included two in this example, but there are a lot more of them. See Section 16.4, page **228** for more information.

Money in (income)
Invoice (accrual)-based business

Date received	Client (customer)	Invoice number	Date of invoice	Bank account received in	Amount received
12/04/20	John Doe	N100	10/03/20	Business	£200

Or if you are a cash business (usually this is people selling a product):

Date	Item (product)	Payment method	Quantity	Cost £	Total £
12/04/20	Ink cartridge	Card	1	8	8

Or you can have a mix of the two tables above.

Invoices out (if applicable)

Date	Client	Invoice number	Payment method	Amount
12/05/20	Mrs Smith	N011	Bank transfer	£100

Each of the above tables (expenses, money in, invoices out) would be on a separate sheet.

 Client: Often used instead of 'customers', particularly in businesses selling services.

 Qty: Short for quantity.

 Sheet: A separate page within a spreadsheet.

STEPS I TAKE TO DO MY BOOKKEEPING

This is just an example of the procedure I personally use to do my bookkeeping. You will have to find what works for you. There are much quicker ways to do bookkeeping.

If you can't access help from an accountant to get a system set up that works for you, many of the organisations offering in-person help (see Section 3.5, page **53**) will have downloadable spreadsheets (you can use a free spreadsheet application, such as Google Sheets).

It took me a long time to learn to do my bookkeeping confidently, and this is the system my mum had used. My parents were not that sure I could do my own bookkeeping, which made me nervous, but I've done it for two and a half years now and it's fine. In the future I will make the switch to something more automated...but not yet.

Expenses – money out

1. Go through Dext on my phone.
2. Type the details of each receipt into the expenses sheet.
3. Go through my bank statement to check there aren't any transactions I have missed.
4. Go through my credit card statement, again to check I've not forgotten to add something to Dext.
5. Add anything that I've missed into Dext.
6. Add items onto the expenses sheet.

Money in – income

1. Look through the incoming monies from my bank statement.
2. Add to the income sheet if there are business monies received.
3. Cross-reference money in with my invoicing system (I use Xero) to get the date of the invoice, customer details and invoice number.
4. Check credit card statement for any income, in case something business related has been refunded and I forgot about it.

Invoices out/written

1. Read list of invoices.
2. Copy details of each invoice into the sheet for outgoing invoices.

BOOKKEEPING ACTIVITY

Abdul and Laura are starting a T-shirt printing business. Below are the transactions for June 2020.

Sort the transactions into income and expenses and add them to the Income and Expenses tables on the next page, and the table of Categories on page **249**. I've filled in the item columns in the Income and Expenses tables and one answer in the Categories table to help you get started, and you can find the answers at the end of the book.

02/06/20	£300 for buying 100 plain T-shirts from Blank TS Ltd
	£25 x 14 local band's T-shirts sold. 7 paid by card, 7 paid cash
	£30 x 20 Blue Sky Thinking T-shirts sold – card
	£12 x 30 Motorbike T-shirts sold – cash
01/06/20	£50 inks from Ink Tastic
11/06/20	£25 water bill from Leeway Water
10/07/20	£80 electricity bill from Light Waves
07/06/20	£25 phone bill from Vodafone
	£30 shipping to customers
20/06/20	£30 shipping customers paid
	£6 insurance with the insurance company

Income

Date	Item	Payment method	Amount	Quantity	Total £
	T-shirt local band				
	T-shirt local band				
	T-shirt Blue Sky Thinking				
	T-shirt Motorbike				
	Shipping costs paid				
Total £					

Expenses

Date	Item	Payment method	Quantity	Unit price	Cost £
	Plain T-shirts				
	Water				
	Electricity				
	Inks				
	Shipping to customers				
	Phone				
	Insurance				
Total £					

Categories

	Stock	Utilities	Shipping	Telecoms	Consumables	Insurance
	300					
Total £	300					

17.5 Review

In this chapter we explored what bookkeeping is and the main ways people do bookkeeping. You found out how I do my bookkeeping, and also did an activity.

ACTION POINTS

Tick in the box when you have completed each action point.

1. Decide on how you will do your bookkeeping. ⬭

2. Set up your bookkeeping system. ⬭

Checklist of things to do next

Item	Done (✓)	Where to get help
Logging receipts and travel/mileage if applicable		Use bookkeeping software, e.g. Dext Business growth hub, online courses
List what you bought for business purposes		Spreadsheet – union or trade organisation in your area may have templates you can download
List sales		How many and what you have sold, or what services you have provided
Invoices for customers, receipts and/or quotes		QuickBooks and other bookkeeping packages, or use Microsoft Word or a paper-based invoice book
Check customers have paid within allotted time as specified on invoice		Check accountancy package – some allow you to set up automatic reminders Spreadsheet or carbon copies of invoices written
Contracts where required		Industry organisation may have templates/guidance
Feedback collection from customers Review feedback and make an action plan for incorporating it into your business		Optional, but can help you work out what you're doing well You can also ask customers if they know of someone they would recommend you to

Common Business Documents

Estimated time to read this chapter: 10 minutes

18.1 What is an invoice and what do you put on it?

An invoice is something you give to customers to say how much they need to pay you for a product or service. For example, I write an invoice for people who book me for training to say how much they need to pay me after I have delivered the training. The basic things invoices need to include are:

- your **business name**, **address** and **logo** (if you have one)
- **company number**, if you have one
- **tax number** for VAT (value-added tax) or GST, if applicable
- **customer's name and address**
- **customer purchase order number** if applicable
- **invoice number**
- **date of invoice**
- **due date** (when you want them to pay you by)
- **unit price** of products/services being bought (how much each item costs, e.g. the unit price for a book might be £12.99)
- **quantity (qty) bought**: how many of the items have been bought
- **item(s) bought**, e.g. books
- **total cost** for the items (e.g. if the customer had bought two books at £12.99, the total cost would be £12.99 + £12.99 = £25.98)
- **how to pay:** If the invoice is created using a bookkeeping package like Xero, it may be possible to give people a web link for them to pay online, or you may prefer people to pay by direct bank transfer or cheque.

What ways are there to make invoices?

- **Word processor**, e.g. Microsoft Word or Google Docs.
- **Invoice book:** Purchasable from stores or online. Invoice books usually create a carbon copy, so there is one copy for you and one for your customer.
- **Spreadsheet software** like Microsoft Excel or Google Sheets.
- **Bookkeeping or accounting software** like QuickBooks or Xero.
- **Handwritten piece of paper.**

18.2 What are receipts, what are they for?

Receipts are used when someone has bought something to prove that the business has received the money. For example, if you sold a book in a book shop, you would probably give the buyer a receipt rather than an invoice. Sometimes if you have provided an invoice, people may also want a receipt to confirm that they have paid and you have received the money. Receipts can be written on a piece of paper.

Ways to write a receipt

- **Receipt book:** Provides a carbon copy of the receipt, so there is one copy for you and one for your customer.
- **Receipt printer:** These can be used with a cash register or card machine, or you can just use regular software like Microsoft Word or Google Docs.
- **Back of business cards**: A common way for taxi drivers to provide receipts is on the back of their business cards.
- **Handwritten piece of paper.**
- **Spreadsheet software.**
- **Bookkeeping and accounting software.**

Quick reference: What you must do to run a business

NOTE: Check what you need to do for benefits/welfare.

ONCE

Register for relevant tax IDs/tax and business numbers (e.g. UK: UTR; Australia: ABN; New Zealand: RealMe login and New Zealand Business Number; Canada: Business Number). ⬜

Register as self-employed if applicable. ⬜

ANNUALLY

Check if you need any licences, permits and insurance and how often they need to be renewed (this changes from time to time, so checking what is required annually is a good idea). ⬜

Renew any relevant permits, licences and insurance. ⬜

Check the laws specific to your industry and follow them. There may, for example, be professional registrations (e.g. if you are working as a counsellor). ⬜

Check if you need insurance for healthcare as well as public liability, etc. ⬜

Pay taxes and any insurance you need. ⬜

Fill in tax return. ⬜

Send/upload (sometimes called lodging or filing) tax return. (NOTE: In some circumstances you may have to give income information more often than once a year.) ⬜

Establish if what you are doing is considered a ⃝
hobby or if you need to register as self-employed.
If you are a limited company then you need to
produce accounts.

Review any forms you will need to fill out at the ⃝
start and end of the year so you can make sure your
monthly records will fit into the relevant forms.

MONTHLY

Keep your receipts from expenses (money spent ⃝
buying things for the business).

Keep a record of services/products you sold to ⃝
customers. You can use receipts or invoices for this.

Pay bills such as electricity, phone, etc. ⃝

Pay for any materials and stock you have bought. ⃝

18.3 What is a business plan?

A business plan is a document that contains information
about your business goals, how you will achieve your goals, and
when you want to achieve them by. Making a business plan can
help you to think about what is important to you, and also how
you will go about getting and keeping customers.

Do you have to have a business plan?
Plenty of self-employed people have started a business
without a plan. You may find a business plan helpful for
clarifying your ideas, and you may need one if you are applying
for funding or benefits, or asking for a loan.

LINKS TO BUSINESS PLAN TEMPLATES

UK

Mutually Inclusive Partnerships For people with learning disabilities (but not exclusively).	www.mutuallyinclusive.co.uk/self-employment.html
Prince's Trust Aimed at young people, but anyone can use the templates.	www.princes-trust.org.uk/help-for-young-people/tools-resources/business-tools/business-plans
British Business Bank You don't have to use their loan service to use their business plan template.	www.startuploans.co.uk/business-planning-templates

USA

US Small Business Administration	www.sba.gov/business-guide/plan-your-business/write-your-business-plan

CANADA

Futurpreneur Canada Support for 18–39-year-olds, but anyone can use the business plan writer for free.	www.futurpreneur.ca/en/resources/start-up-business-planning/tips-tools/business-plan writer
Business Development Bank of Canada (BDC)	www.bdc.ca/en/articles-tools/start-buy-business/start-business/pages/create-effective-business-plan.aspx?type=B&order=1&intlnk=rightbox

AUSTRALIA

Australian Government website	www.business.gov.au/planning/ business-plans/how-to-develop- your-business-plan

NEW ZEALAND

New Zealand Government website	www.anz.co.nz/business/bizhub/ start/how-to-write-a-simple- business-plan www.business.govt.nz/ getting-started/business- planning-tools-and-tips/ how-to-write-a-business-plan

If the online business plan templates feel a bit overwhelming or long, I have created a one-page business plan template which you can use to help you to think about writing a business plan.

Example business plan

My business name/logo is

Marks Deliveries

My customers' needs are/they are interested in

getting their things delivered on time and safety.

My customers will live/work/purchase

locally, but might book my services online.

I will sell/provide	**It will cost**
packing of goods, such as when moving to a new house, and delivering them safely.	40p per mile I £10 per hour of my time

I am different to my competitors because

my van is electric powered, so I appeal to eco-conscious customers.

I will collect customer feedback by

asking people to recommend me on Google Maps and asking for verbal feedback.

I will write my invoices with	**I will write receipts**
QuickBooks.	on the back of business cards.

I will do my bookkeeping using	**My accountant will be**
QuickBooks.	Joseph Alexandra.

Five people I can ask for help are

1 My friend who is self-employed
2 Dad, who is good at maths
3 Union helpline
4 My auntie, who is very sensible
5 My business advisor

BUSINESS PLAN

My business name/logo is

My customers' needs are/they are interested in

My customers will live/work/purchase

I will sell/provide   It will cost

I am different to my competitors because

I will collect customer feedback by

I will write my invoices with   I will write receipts

I will do my bookkeeping using   My accountant will be

Five people I can ask for help are

18.4 One more thing

Before finishing this chapter, you should also have in the
back of your mind that you should start saving a bit of money
each month. Even if it's only £1, it is better than nothing. It
is important to do this because you will have times where not
much money is coming into your business, but you still have
to pay rent, bills, etc., and you also need to be able to support
yourself if you get ill or take a holiday (even if you just take
a few days off without going anywhere). Also, from time
to time things will go wrong, equipment will break or you'll
need supplies like ink cartridges for your printer to finish a
piece of work. You need the money to be able to pay for these
things – you can't tell a client that you're sorry you can't do a
piece of work this week as you don't have enough money for
ink cartridges (well you could, but the client probably wouldn't
be very happy). This is part of cash flow; see Section 21.4,
page **288** for more information.

18.5 Review

In this chapter you learnt what an invoice and receipt are,
what information they need to have on them, and how you can
make your own. You also learnt about business plans.

ACTION POINTS

Tick in the box when you have completed each action point.

1. If applicable, decide how you will make invoices and design your invoice template. ☐

2. Read through the checklists on what you need to do to run a business. ☐

3. (Optional) Write a business plan. ☐

PART 7

Day-to-Day Running of a Business

Aims: In Part 7 we will explore the day-to-day things you need to do to run a business.

19

Buying Stock for Your Business

19.1 How do you buy things for your business?

In this chapter I am specifically talking about businesses that are buying stock and/or raw materials to make products.

> **?** **Buyer:** In this context, a person who is responsible for choosing and purchasing stock or materials for a business.

> **?** **Bulk buy:** To buy a lot of something. This may cost you less money per item than if you bought only one item at a time – this is common with wholesalers.

> **?** **Stock:** In this context, I am generally referring to physical things you can sell, not the stock market, stocks and shares, etc.

Wholesalers and distributors are both businesses that mainly sell to other businesses. You can usually find industry-specific wholesalers and distributors in trade magazines.

19.2 Ways to pay

Sale or return: This means that when you buy stock, after an agreed/set amount of time (term), for example 30 days, you can either return the stock to the supplier or pay for it. This gives you some protection if you are unsure of how a product will sell, because if it doesn't sell you can just give it back. This won't work for all products or materials you use to make products.

Term in this context is the details of an agreement, e.g. how many days you can have a product before having to pay for or return it.

Business/trade accounts: You can sometimes get a 'trade account' with a supplier. This makes ordering easier as they give you an account number which links to your details on their customer database, so you don't have to keep telling the supplier your address and other details each time you order.

Pay on invoice: This means that rather than paying up front, i.e. when you order the stock, you pay for it after you receive the invoice. The invoice will give a due date, which is the date you must pay the invoice by (e.g. 30 days after the invoice is sent). This can also be helpful for managing cash flow.

19.3 What is manufacturing?

 Manufacturing: The term usually used when multiples of the same product are made from raw materials, e.g. in a factory.

Some businesses will design a product and then pay a factory to make the product; this could be anything from cushions to computer technology. Depending on the manufacturer you use, you may have to source and buy your own raw materials and get them shipped to the manufacturer. Once the products have been made, they are then shipped to you or your customers.

Source means to find something. For example, a prop maker for a theatre might be asked to source headlights for a car they are making as a prop.

Shipped in this context means delivered to you. This could be by ship, road, boat, etc.

If you are getting things manufactured in a country that you do not live in, then the products will be imported into the country you live in and this may incur extra costs. This is outside the remit of this book.

19.4 Review

In this chapter we covered the basic terminology often used when buying products as a business, including payment terms (e.g. sale or return, pay on invoice), and how this can help manage the cash flow of your business.

ACTION POINTS

Tick in the box when you have completed each action point.

1. Plan how you will buy products, materials or anything else you will need for your business. ◯

2. Research possible suppliers if applicable. ◯

20

Networking

20.1 What is networking?

Networking can mean different things in different contexts. In computing, networking means connecting computers together, with physical wires or via the internet or Bluetooth, or another connection method. The goal of networking in computing is to enable the computers to share information and resources, such as printers and memory.

Networking in a business context usually means connecting people together. Being connected means being able to talk to someone, for example on Facebook, via e-mail, on the phone, or seeing a person in real life. Networking is not just about getting work. Networking is also about people being aware of who you are and what you do. For example, how would you know that there are companies that sell ink cartridges compatible with major brands of printers if you had not heard of or seen them?

20.2 How to make new connections

You could make connections at networking events, or just talking to people in everyday life. This will vary depending on the industry you work in.

 Industry: An industry in this context refers to the type of work you do. For example, if you made fashionable clothes, you'd be working in the fashion industry. If you were a factory owner, you would be working in the manufacturing industry.

In the survey I did for the research for this book, people said that networking was difficult for them. I did a follow-up survey about networking with 51 autistic people. In this survey I also asked about people's area of work; they were diverse, including barristers, education professionals and IT professionals. Fifty per cent of people worked either as writers or journalists.

You need to choose places to network that are compatible with your needs (see the access/needs audit in Section 3.8, page **59**).

'I go to conferences and other events related to the work I do, where I talk to people at the food/drinks table and the stalls, and after the talks/presentations.' (**Robyn**)

'I also network by asking people on my feedback form if they know anywhere else I could speak to.' (**Robyn**)

'I am very social and prefer face-to-face communication or the phone. When I work on projects, I meet fellow freelancers.' (**Robyn**)

20.3 How to maintain connections

It's good to meet people, but the next stage is for you to be mutually beneficial to each other, which strengthens the connection. This does not have to mean doing work for free, but might be listening to each other's ideas, and coming up with projects you can work together on.

When communicating with anyone in a business/self-employment capacity, make sure to be polite, finishing your e-mails with 'Kind regards' or similar. Be courteous – say 'please' if asking for something and 'thank you' if someone has helped you. This may seem obvious, but with e-mail being so quick and everyone being so busy, your politeness can really affect people's attitudes towards you.

E-mailing periodically via an e-newsletter can be a really great and easy way of maintaining connections.

When thinking about maintaining connections, consider why someone might want to stay connected to you, i.e. what is the person getting from you that is of value to them? (See the explanation of values in Section 11.2, page **157**.) (NOTE: I do not mean money when talking about value in this context.)

20.4 How to make the most of connections

Making the most of connections is about looking for opportunities. This could be a sale (in business speak this is called a conversion), or it could be finding a project that you could work together on (and both be paid for). It could also be making sure that you are as helpful to each other as is possible (without the balance being too unequal, or negatively impacting you).

20.5 How to evaluate connections

Drawing a connection map and reviewing it once a year might help you to evaluate your connections, and assess if you are making the most of the energy you have. Many autistic people find socialising costs a lot of energy. Networking and maintaining your network should not be negatively impacting you so much you are unable to work.

If you feel like networking is not benefiting you and you are just collecting connections, then you may want to think about what you would want to get out of networking.

Here are some questions to think about:

- Who are you currently networking with?
- How are you networking?

- Are there ways of maintaining connections that cost less energy? An example of this may be an e-newsletter (you could use a website like Mailchimp to help you do this).

20.6 Real-life examples of how networking works

On the next few pages, I provide three examples of people within my network. First of all, I should say that I am a very sociable person. If you do not like socialising or find it difficult to socialise, you could consider a partnership business structure (see Section 15.2, page **208**) with someone who has the skills you don't have (but doesn't have the skills you do have).

I think of networking as something which happens all the time. For me it's just about being friendly and beneficial to each other. Good examples of this follow.

- *Ben Connors: artist*
  Ben and I have been friends for about 12 years. When you look at our timeline (page **273**), it wasn't until we had been friends for six years that we started doing something that earned money.

- *Heart n Soul: arts organisation*
  Heart n Soul is an arts organisation based in south-east London. They believe in the power and talents of people with learning disabilities, and autistic people.

- *Sarah Jane Critchley: author, trainer and coach*
  Sarah Jane worked for the Autism Education Trust for ten years. Sarah Jane supports me to manage clients who have a lot of forms that need to be filled in. I do not earn money through Sarah Jane, but she enables

me to earn money. Notice the gap of eight years before I worked directly with her. In that eight years I didn't do too much to maintain our connection. I just made a point of saying hello and being nice, not because I wanted anything but just because I want to be nice to others and learn from other people.

TIMELINE NOTE: The £ signs indicate that I got paid.

ROBYN AND BEN'S CONNECTION TIMELINE (THIS IS JUST SOME OF THE HIGHLIGHTS)

2008	We met at a campaign event.	
2009	Ben was running a club night with a friend. They invited me to play.	
2009	Went to see Ben DJ.	
2011	Visited Ben's stall at a Christmas market.	
2014	Ben introduced me to Heart n Soul.	
2015	Worked with Ben as an arts assistant at an event.	£
2015	Helped Ben run a comic workshop.	£
2015	Delivered training for an art museum on autism with Ben.	£
2015-2017	Worked with Ben to help make an art gallery more accessible.	£
2017	Helped Ben plan a project working with young autistic people.	
2017	Ben invited me to be a guest on his radio show.	
2017	Played at Ben's art show.	
2018	Ben invited me to be on Worldwide Radio with him.	
2019	Worked with Ben on a project called Heart n Soul at The Hub.	

HEART N SOUL

2014	Invited to play a gig.	
2015	Worked with Ben as assistant at an event.	£
2016	Time in studio.	
2016	Ran a screen-printing workshop.	£
2016	Started working on an application for a research residency.	
2017	Became part of the artist development programme.	£
2017	Played a gig at a local theatre.	
2017	Invited to speak at a local event.	£
2017	Invited to speak at an event in Hull.	£
2018	Started working at a residency.	£
2020	Became a creative associate.	£

When I agreed to work on the application for the residency it was with the agreement that I would be paid for a certain amount of days for the length of the project, which was two years if we were successful. It was a risk, but I felt like I would benefit from the process of doing the application. I enjoyed it. And it connected me to people I did not know before.

SARAH JANE

2008	Met Sarah Jane at autism-related events.
2016	Sarah Jane was on the interview panel for the autism programme board which I sat on for a year.
2018	Asked Sarah Jane if she would work with me to manage some of my larger clients as I struggled to communicate with them.
2020	Paid Sarah Jane to proofread my website.

20.7 How you could network

There are a lot of different ways of networking. Hopefully you can find one that is compatible with your needs and strengths. Some ways of doing it are described below. Each industry will have its own characteristics, so you may need to adapt these.

Union and other industry organisation events
This could include small training events with just a few people, one-to-one business sessions, or large conferences or exhibitions (expos). If you are at a lecture or a similar event, and you feel able to ask a question (making it as interesting as possible), when it's your turn to speak you could say something like...

'Hi, my name is... I am a writer for (name of newspaper or organisation) and I'd like to ask...'

'Attend networking events that are specific to your work or that have a higher likelihood of hosting *actual* potential customers, rather than larger, generic events. Also, check the attendee list beforehand to find a handful of specific people you would most like to connect with.' (**Research participant**)

If you stand out, you can use this to your advantage. I have what is called prosopagnosia, which means I am unable to recognise faces, so I rely on people recognising me. I wear a purple hat and purple glasses, and usually Doc Martens boots, so I am recognisable. This way, rather than looking odd and rude for not recognising people, I just look different and memorable.

Speed networking events

Speed networking events are good if you can handle being in a noisy room, and only like to talk to people for short amounts of time.

In a speed networking event, people are seated across from each other and speak to the person sat across from them about their business for a set amount of time, for example five minutes. When the time is up, people move to a different seat and speak to someone new. This is a good format if you find it difficult to know what to say, as you can practise what you are going to say before the event. When planning what to say, maybe aim for a 15-to-30-second introduction. Try to include, for example:

- your first name and business name
- what you do
- the last most interesting piece of work you did, summed up in one or two sentences

You could also give them a business card.

After the other person has given their introduction, you would spend the rest of the time asking each other questions about what you each said in your introduction, or other topics of common interest. The goal here is to form a positive lasting impression on each other, not necessarily to sell anything.

Here is an example:

   'Hi, my name is Femi. What's your name?'

Then you could say:

   'I am a writer and blogger. My last piece was about highlighting the experiences of women in construction jobs.'

Then you could say:

'What do you do?'

Ask questions about what they say even if you are not that interested, as it demonstrates you were listening.

At the end of the conversation you might say:

   'Here is my card. Do you have a card?'
(This refers to business cards.)

Networking online

If you are someone who struggles with social interaction face to face, you can network online. There are lots of methods to do this – for example:

- **forums**, e.g. of any industry bodies, unions, etc. you are a member of
- **social media**, like Facebook groups or other online gatherings of people, such as LinkedIn, which is like Facebook but for professionals.
  Focus on not just getting likes but also good-quality interaction.

 Good-quality interaction is when it feels like you're having more of a conversation about the things you post/share rather than people just liking it or tagging someone else they think may be interested.

Online events can also be a great way to connect with others. You can use the chat function to ask questions within this format. It may not be appropriate to say 'Hi, I'm Noel from Notebook Solutions', for example, but when you sign up for these events, you can choose your display name to be your business name or your name (not things like Adam's iPad).

People will see your name pop up on screen when you ask a question, and over time if you're asking good questions that are interesting to others, people will start to remember you.

'I always use online platforms to form relationships in a "safe" and controllable environment, so I feel they can get to know me in a way they might not face to face because of my shyness, and so on.' (**Research participant**)

It is not just about selling

If you are passionate about what your business does/sells/ provides, this will help you, because basically networking is having conversations about topics that interest you and the person you are speaking to. Don't focus on selling (sometimes called converting) during face-to-face interactions at networking events – try to enjoy learning about other people.

Converting means when someone who is interested in what your business offers decides to buy something from you.

Use sensory adaptations

You might find sunglasses and ear plugs useful (you can get mouldable silicone clear ear plugs that people won't be able to see you're wearing unless they get very close to your ear). Don't be afraid to do what you need to; you wouldn't expect a wheelchair user to not use their wheelchair because of what other people may think.

Learn from other people

Listen to what others say when they network: how do they move the conversation forward, how long do they speak for, what kinds of questions do they ask? Many autistic people are good at systemising — now is a great time to use this skill.

Make sure you rest afterwards

If networking makes you tired, make sure you rest afterwards, and try to do networking on a day without other commitments when possible.

If you have the energy to do so the following week, day or month, it's good to reconnect with people you have met at events, as when you meet a lot of people it is easy to forget people. Giving people a call to action — for example, 'Here is a link to my website' — gives you an opportunity to start a conversation later — for example, 'What did you think of my website?'

 'I have learned to book an extra day when I travel to an event so that I can just lie on my back in the hotel with the drapes closed before I have to get on a plane again.' **(Research participant)**

You don't have to stay for the whole event. Even if you're only there for ten minutes, that's better than not having gone at all.

Do not be afraid to disclose that you are autistic to event organisers and/or people you network with. It should always be an individual's choice as to when and to whom they disclose being autistic, and you should never feel pressure to do this. You could use soft disclosure, a term often used by Temple Grandin. For example, you could tell the network event organiser, 'I am sensitive to light and wondered what the lighting will be like at your event?' Or if you find social skills hard when networking, you could say:

 'Hi, I'm…and I am autistic. I find socialising hard, so if I am rude or talk too much please tell me.'

'I'm openly autistic, so that cuts out those who don't wish to take me at face value. I often speak to organisers prior and explain that I find it difficult to initiate conversations (I'm also selective mute which doesn't help), so often I get to do a two-minute pitch at the beginning of events where I can explain what I do, and also explain that I struggle to approach people. People usually come to me after that, so I know that they are interested in what I'm doing, which makes conversation easier.' (**Research participant**)

Networking is a skill you have to learn and practise, but is something you can improve on.

 'Go with someone who is good at networking and stick by their side.' (**Research participant**)

 'I prefer to attend networking events with a person I feel comfortable with so I can follow their lead.' (**Research participant**)

If you're at an event and you know someone, ask them to introduce you to someone you don't know.

 'Look for sociable networking events in your area, e.g. Jelly, Likemind, as they are more supportive and less competitive.' (**Research participant**)

NETWORKING LINKS

Jelly is an informal event where self-employed or small business owners can meet and chat with other small business owners.

www.uk-jelly.org.uk (search for events in your area at http://wiki.workatjelly.com/w/page/12752597/FrontPage)

Likemind is an app that allows you to make a social media-type account as well as share things in listings like Craigslist or Gumtree.	www.likemind.com

You do not have to go to a 'networking event' to network

Networking can happen anywhere. If you are working in the arts you may not go to specific networking events, but instead go to events based around your interests/business, for example a writers' circle, where writers read aloud or read each other's work and critique it (each writer's circle is different).

You might also find yourself networking at non-business events, for example at events at your church, mosque, synagogue or temple, or at local community events. If something related to your business comes up in conversation, don't be afraid to ask the person if they would like your business card.

20.8 Review

In this chapter we explored what networking is, and different ways in which people network. We explored why networking can be helpful, and how its focus should not just be about sales. We looked at example timelines of connections in my network, and also read quotes from people who participated in my research survey for this book.

ACTION POINTS

Tick in the box when you have completed each
action point.

1. List some strategies you think you would find
    helpful at networking events. ☐

2. Do some online research to find some networking
    events that you might enjoy. They could be online
    events, small in-person events, or events related
    to your business but that are not technically
    networking, e.g. a writer's circle. ☐

Getting Paid for Your Work

Estimated time to read this chapter: 20 minutes

21.1 Terminology

In this chapter we are specifically thinking about you being paid for products or services you provide or sell. I have used the word **cash** in this chapter. Cash means different things in different contexts, so let's just review the different meanings of cash and related terms as they apply in different contexts.

> **?** **Cash:** As a means of payment, 'cash' means physical money. In the UK it may be called notes and coins; other parts of the world may refer to it as 'bills' (dollar bills, not your electricity bill).

> **?** **Cash flow** means money going in and out of the business. For example, as a business you pay bills (that's cash going out) and you receive cash when a customer pays you. You can read more about cash flow in Section 21.4, page 288.

On a US tax form, you will see a check box for 'Cash' and 'Accrual'. Cash in this context means when your customers pay on the day that they buy from you or receive your service, even if it takes time for the money to arrive in your bank.

A business can receive (sometimes called **receivables** in bookkeeping/accounting software) both cash and accrual payments.

In **funding application budgets**, cash is money you have or will have, as opposed to support in kind, which has a value but is not money in your bank account (such as when someone offers you reduced cost for products or services, or help for free). If you can ever see it on your bank statement, it's cash. Obviously, there may be some funders who work out project budgets differently, so be sure to read the documentation around the funding or contact the potential funder for more information.

21.2 What to expect when getting paid

You don't always get paid as quickly as you hope you will. If you are providing a service, I would highly recommend using a contract (see Section 21.6, page **294** for more details).

How can customers/clients pay your business?
There are a few ways that you can be paid. In this chapter I will go into detail about the main ways, but some possible methods are:

- cash
- cheques
- credit/debit card
- PayPal
- bank transfer
- web platforms, e.g. Etsy, eBay
- pay on invoice (technically not a payment method, but an important concept to understand).

21.3 Cash flow when working with accrual customers/clients

Paying on invoice (sometimes known as accrual) is when a customer pays after you have delivered the product or service. Usually you would use a purchase order or contract to formally agree payment terms. Often, the bigger the organisation you are dealing with, the longer it will take them to pay you. If a client pays invoices 30 days after receiving the invoice, you will have to wait that long to get the money in your bank. This can cause problems with cash flow if you do not plan for it. Note that sometimes the payment term will be for a number of **working days**, i.e. excluding weekends and bank/public holidays, so you would have to wait even longer.

EXAMPLE

Jane and Sara run a cleaning business. They clean offices, and invoice their clients. If they send out their invoices at the end of May and the payment terms in the purchase order are 30 days (which is quite common), then at the beginning of June they will still be waiting to get paid. In the meantime, though, they need to replenish their Henry Hoover bags and toilet bleach, as well as paying their overheads such as their phone and internet bill. If they pay all these bills at once they may get to the point where there is no money in their bank account, as they are still waiting for their clients to pay. This means that they can't work as they have no bags for Henry Hoover, or bleach for toilets. They would have to wait till at least the end of June to be able to buy more hoover bags and bleach to be able to work again; in the meantime their clients may start using a different provider for their cleaning needs.

 Purchase order: A formal document setting out work to be completed, and responsibilities of the seller and buyer.

You may think this is a very simple problem to solve – you just make sure you have enough of everything – but I wanted to keep this example simple so that it is easy to understand. Cash flow has been the reason lots of large businesses fail; you need money to flow into and out of the business.

This is not just important for accrual-based businesses. For example, when customers pay by card, it can often take a day or two, or sometimes longer, for the money to go into your bank account. If you have bills that need to be paid while you are waiting for this payment, then this can cause a cash flow problem.

There are plenty of strategies you can use to manage cash flow.

21.4 Managing cash flow

Overdraft: Money a bank loans to you on a temporary basis. You usually have to apply for an overdraft in advance of needing it. An overdraft costs money (often a fee and some interest). This is OK in an emergency, but should be avoided where possible.

Interest: A percentage charged (usually monthly) on money you owe (such as a loan).

Credit cards: You can use a credit card to buy stock or other items without having the money at that time. If you pay it back soon enough (e.g. at the end of each month), you won't usually be charged interest. This is useful if you know a customer will be paying you the money in time for you to pay the credit card company before you get charged interest. I do this, but I speak to a few trusted people if I am trying to make a decision. This is something you should probably only do when you absolutely know you will be paid.

 Deposit: A deposit is when a client/customer pays an amount of their overall fee up front, i.e. before you give them the product or service, as opposed to paying the whole fee they owe on receipt of invoice. Alternatively, sometimes deposits are used when loaning or leasing something, for example a bicycle shop may ask for a deposit of $10 when someone hires a bike, and the customer will be given their $10 back when they return the bicycle they hired.

Balance sheet

One tool you can use to help manage cash flow is a balance sheet. A template of a balance sheet will be available from most of the organisations that offer in-person help (see page **53**) with starting a business. But if you find numbers difficult, you need to make a plan. Below are some steps that may help you.

Calculating core costs

Core costs is how much money you have to pay out each month just to keep the business going – for example, for electricity, internet. Work out how much this is each month, and try to always keep this amount in your bank account if possible. Ideally, keep a few months' worth of core costs available.

Look for patterns

In the first year or two of being self-employed you will learn a lot. You should start to see patterns. For example, for me there isn't usually any training work in August or

December, so I know I need to ensure I am using other revenue streams to keep the cash flowing through my business in those months.

Speak to other self-employed people who do similar things to you, to understand when things might be busy or slow for you, and consider if you could add more revenue streams to bring in money in the slow times. There may also be times when you have to work longer hours than you would like to make sure there is enough money for the quiet (slow) months.

Save money

Put money by, and invest in the business in busy times, to ensure you have enough materials, fuel, etc. to get you through the slow times.

Tax bill

Don't forget to save money towards your tax bill. In the UK, whilst my business year ends in March, I have to pay my tax bill between October and December. When you first start as a self-employed person your tax bill may only be small, but it can grow. One way to control this is to spend what otherwise would be profit in the business, helping it to grow, for example adding more revenue streams or buying large quantities of stock (which might get you a discount). This reduces your tax bill because you have spent the money on things that are tax deductible.

One reason for having an accountant is that they can tell you how much your tax bill will be months in advance, so you can prepare for it.

In the UK if your tax bill is more than £1000 you will start being charged tax twice a year.

COUNTRY-SPECIFIC INFORMATION

UK

If you are seeking payment from large businesses/ organisations you may be asked to fill out questions relating to IR35. IR35 is a piece of law which aims to protect people who work for companies to make sure they get what they are entitled to, such as holiday pay. Some large companies set up small companies or say that their workers are self-employed when they are not, so they don't have to give employees sick pay, holiday pay, etc.

To prove to a company that you are self-employed for tax you might need to provide your UTR (unique taxpayer reference) or company number, and VAT (value-added tax) number if you are VAT registered. You may also need public liability insurance. They may ask you to fill in a 'new supplier' form. This might be in a physical form, or digital form, or involve inputting details into the organisation's computer system via an online form. (You may find this link useful: www. gov.uk/employment-status/selfemployed-contractor.)

> **Public liability insurance:** If, when you are working with people (e.g. running workshops), someone was to get hurt and sued you, you could claim on the public liability insurance.

USA

If you are doing a piece of work for an organisation they may ask you to fill in a W9 tax declaration. This is a form that details your address, social security number, etc. This should ensure the right amount of tax gets taken from the right person.

21.5 More details about payment methods

Invoice

See Section 18.1, page **253** for more information.

Cash

Some businesses are more cash based (normally when customers are spending relatively small amounts of money). Examples could be market stalls and car washes.

Some bank accounts charge you to pay cash into your account.

Credit/debit card

There are two main ways to take credit/debit card payments:

1. You can take out a contract with a credit card merchant services provider (often a bank), and set up a payment gateway, which connects your website to a payment processing network.

2. You can use a mobile payment device, like SumUp, Square (sometimes called Square Up) and iZettle. These offer a small mobile credit card machine that can fit in your pocket. It connects via Bluetooth to your phone or tablet (you can also buy ones that connect to the internet via a sim card). Customers can tap (pay wave, contactless pay, etc.) their card, or insert it and type in their pin either on their tablet or phone or on the credit card machine itself. You can buy ones that have a receipt printer built into it, or you can use an external receipt printer (i.e. a receipt printer that connects, usually via Bluetooth, to the mobile card machine).

Mobile card machine companies usually charge a percentage

per transaction. The percentage taken varies, but is usually between 1.5 and 2.75%. Many of the companies just deposit the money for the products/services sold into your bank account minus the percentage, but some may send you a monthly bill. You should check with the different providers of mobile card machines to find out how the arrangement works.

These kinds of systems work well for small purchases, but for bigger purchases they can cost you a lot, in which case a different payment method may be more suitable.

Cheque

A cheque is a piece of paper that represents money, with your name or your business name on it. Cheques can be paid into a bank account, but if you have a business bank account (you can run a business without a business bank account if you are a sole trader), you may have to pay a fee to pay a cheque in. Cheques need to have the name that is on the bank account they are being paid in to written or printed on them. For example, if a customer wanted to pay by cheque and wrote it to your business name, you would be unable to pay it into your personal account.

It is good practice to ask customers to write a contact telephone number, e-mail address or postal address on the back of their cheque in case you need to contact them, for example if there is a problem when paying the cheque in.

Bank transfer

Different countries have different systems to transfer money between different bank accounts. The system used in the UK is BACS (Bankers Automated Payment System).

International transfer

If you are transferring money internationally you can use an international bank account number (IBAN) and

SWIFT (Society for the Worldwide Interbank Financial Telecommunication) code.

PayPal
PayPal is a very popular method for payment. It allows you to put money in a virtual wallet and pay other people who have a PayPal account.

Web payments
Different platforms, like Etsy, eBay and Bandcamp, will use different ways to get money to you. Before deciding to use a platform, you should read their website information about web payments. Also make sure you check how much you have to pay per transaction.

21.6 What to do if a customer doesn't pay or pays late

Sometimes you just have to keep e-mailing or calling, or get someone else to do it.

Within your contract or purchase order should be payment terms, including a late payment fee. You can challenge a client/customer who has not paid their invoice through the small claims court. To do this you need a contract between you and your customer. You can usually get contract templates from your trade union (see Section 12.2, page **166** for details) or from in-person help (see Section 3.5, page **53**). If you are really stuck, you could use an online service like www.rocketlawyer.com.

Don't let people get away with not paying you, especially if they do it more than once or it is for large sums of money.

If customers are not paying you what they agreed to, this is basically the same as stealing. Do not let people get away with this. Even if not for yourself, if you don't let them get away with it, they will be less likely to try not paying other self-employed people.

You could also consider asking for a deposit. This could be used to buy the materials you need to fulfil your customer's order. But it also gives you safety – asking for a deposit can deter people who are trying to take advantage of you, because you are demonstrating that you're not a pushover. (I know this might seem a bit confusing, as many autistic people are honest and wouldn't dream of not paying someone.)

See page **222** for more information on why contracts are so important.

COUNTRY-SPECIFIC RESOURCES

UK

GOV.UK Making a court claim for money	www.gov.uk/ make-court-claim-for-money
Ministry of Justice See Civil Procedure Rules Part 27	www.justice.gov.uk/courts/ procedure-rules/civil/rules

USA

Search online for your state + 'small claims court'.

CANADA

Canadian Bar Association	www.cba.org

AUSTRALIA

Australian Competition and Consumer Commission	www.accc.gov.au

NEW ZEALAND

Dispute Tribunal of New Zealand	https://disputestribunal.govt.nz

21.7 Review

In this chapter we looked at the different ways customers could pay you, including how customers could pay by card, and also what to do if a customer does not pay you.

ACTION POINTS

Tick in the box when you have completed each action point.

1. Review the payment options that other businesses similar to yours use. ☐

2. Research how much it will cost to use the payment services you think will be most suitable for your business. ☐

3. If applicable, make an action plan for how you will get a contract template, when you will use a contract and what your payment terms will be. ☐

PART 8

Self-Employment Stories

Madge the piano teacher

Who is Madge?

Madge is in her forties and lives in Sheffield, a city in Yorkshire in the north of England. She was diagnosed autistic as an adult and teaches piano in three schools and in her studio. She has one guinea pig, owns her own house and lives with her wife. They met through a dating advert in a newspaper. In 2019 Madge was awarded an Autism-Friendly Business Award from the National Autistic Society. Madge is part of a theatre group. She also gets invited to play the organ at a local church.

What led Madge to decide to become self-employed?

Madge describes herself as almost a selective mute during her school years. She started piano lessons when she was five, and is passionate about music.

After school she studied music at Cambridge University and then moved on to a teaching qualification. Towards the end of her training her fellow classmates were getting jobs in school, but she couldn't get past the interviews, so she decided to start her own business and teach the piano.

How did Madge start working as a piano teacher?

When she first started being self-employed, she did a course that was provided free of charge. The course offered cash incentives if you made the business successful. She placed an advert in a shop (store) window to get pupils, and bought her piano by replying to an ad she saw in a shop window.

She communicates with other teachers online if she has a question about how to best help one of her students. She also answers other teachers' questions on an online forum. Most of Madge's students come from word-of-mouth referrals.

Where does Madge work?

Madge has a studio in a small business centre a short walk from her home, which she found when walking past it. The business centre is not an office block, but looks more like some houses that have been knocked together. As you enter through a wooden gate there is a gazebo above you, and lots of benches and picnic tables for people to sit down. There is an outdoor pizza oven, cafe and bar. There are a guitar tutor, music equipment hire, barbers and many more businesses at the centre.

To get to the studio you have to walk through the barber's shop. The studio has calming green walls with canvas photos on the wall of Bob Marley and another photo of some stones. She has an electric upright piano in her studio and at home. Previously she was in a studio within a former school which is at the end of her street.

Since 2020, Madge has also taught classes online.

What kind of students does Madge teach?

Her pupils range from children to adults. Her eldest is in their 80s. Some of her students want to do grades, but others just want to enjoy music. For these pupils, Madge makes arrangements of pop songs, or whatever genre the student is interested in.

She sends out invoices half termly and does her bookkeeping each week.

 Half term: In the UK the school year is split into three terms. About halfway through each term, there is a week-long (sometimes two-week-long) holiday, which is called half term.

Niche Comics

What is Niche Comics?
Niche Comics is a comic- and bookshop in the town of Huntingdon in the east of England. It's run by two brothers, Adam and Guy.

What is the shop like?
The shop was built in 1570 and Guy tells me that the back door, which seems two feet too short, is that way because when the building was built, the higher the door, the more tax you paid.

A bell gently dings as you enter the shop and I was instantly put at ease by the spread of genres and styles of books on the table, with authors whose names I recognised, such as Lauren Child (who illustrated and wrote the book and TV series *Charlie and Lola*), and Matt Haig, as well as a book explaining in pictures what politics is and a book that is black and about colours (it uses Braille and texture to communicate). I guess I was imagining rows of comic books (which I struggle to read because of my poor sight), but was glad to see lots of children's books and adults' books, and greetings cards in a rack. There is a neatly laid out wall of comics, including one that is on the theme of love and LGBT (lesbian, gay, bisexual and transgender) rights, the profits of which go to the victims of the Orlando nightclub attack in 2016. Further into the shop there is a whole section dedicated to Warhammer, including a four-foot (at least) tall display of paint for the figures. Next to this section is the short door, and this leads out to a courtyard/garden with a bench and flowers. This is where the brothers host local musicians to give them a chance to play somewhere without the usual distractions you get at a gig.

Upstairs in the shop are two rooms. One is the children's section, with childhood favourites like *The Tiger Who Came to*

Tea and *The Very Hungry Caterpillar*. In the centre of the room is a small table with a brightly coloured range of seating options. On one of the chairs are some cuddly toys, including two sloths. The room next to the children's section has graphic novels. One of Guy's favourites is *The Sandman*. There are also more traditional books like Lee Child's novels.

Throughout the shop you can hear music playing. When I was there it was Motown classics.

The brothers also have a stall they take to events like Comic-Con International.

When I visited it was my second face-to-face interview for this book, and I was struck by how Madge, Adam and Guy all mentioned how difficult interviews had been when applying for jobs, and how draining social interaction can be. This is why the brothers take it in turns to be in the shop – it gives each of them time to recoup their energy.

What is the area around the shop like?
The shop is at the less busy end of the high street. This end street is somewhat set aside from the busier half by a marketplace and church. The kind of shops in the high street include chain cafe shops, and cards and stationery shops. Next door to Niche Comics on the left is a pub, and next door on the right is an estate agents. The brothers are both in the shop on Mondays and then take it in turns the other days of the week.

What led Guy and Adam (shop owners) to become self-employed?
Adam has a degree in philosophy, but like many autistic people found getting a job after university very difficult. Guy worked in several low-skilled jobs, like working in the canteen of a local company and another at a meat processing plant, before running the shop with Adam.

Both Adam and Guy have a keen interest in comics. Guy

tells me he started reading *The Beano* as a child and later the superhero comics like *Superman*.

Their mum was able to help them buy their shop with some inheritance money.

How did they start the business?
Adam and Guy attended a short two-week course on running a business. This course was provided by Business Link, a business advice and guidance service, and it gave them an overview of what they needed to do to run a shop. They began with just the first room in the shop, selling comics, and over the last eight years have expanded the range of books and comics they sell. When I was there, they had customers even though it was a rainy Monday afternoon. They also have each other.

Francie the jeweller

Who is Francie?
Francie is a mum to two kids.

Francie works from home in San Francisco. Her neighbourhood, like much of San Francisco, has lots of hills, and the Muni (streetcar) is not far away from where she lives. She is also not too far from the ocean. Her house is modern and very typical for the area; on the second floor there is her kitchen and main living space. She offers me popcorn and a choice of straw for my drink. We sit down in her living room with her dog, who is very friendly.

How did Francie become self-employed?
Francie made jewellery as a child, at first at the beach. People told her that it's really hard to be a jewellery maker, so she started designing jewellery for other jewellery makers; then she started working in a bead store, where she was given the

responsibility to book people to run workshops in the store. When Francie's first child was born, the sensory experience was overwhelming. Her daughter would scratch her face to try and regulate her sensory experiences. Francie needed jewellery that could meet both her and her daughter's sensory needs. She designed jewellery that could be worn safely around the neck and that both mother and baby could play with. This was how her line Lullaby Links started. She has another line of jewellery called Fancy Fidget.

How did Francie find customers?

To begin with Francie wasn't sure how to find her customers, but then she was introduced to a group of parents who were interested in baby wraps (a way of carrying your baby close to you). The parents would spend US$50–100 on a good wrap, and Francie realised they could be her customers too.

She now employs people to work with her when needed to assemble her jewellery. She uses a range of tools, including a small red blow torch. She works with silver and gold; the gold comes in rolls.

Creativity Explored

What is Creativity Explored?

Creativity Explored is an artist's studio and gallery space for artists with developmental disabilities (i.e. intellectual/learning/autistic).

Building and location

Creativity Explored is based in the Mission District of San Francisco. Their building has wood on the front but is made from concrete, and it has big windows either side of the building that form a small corridor, leading to a porch in the shape of an arc at the door.

The gallery space has wooden flooring, and recessed lighting in the ceiling. There is a counter on the left as you go in. As well as selling their artists' work, they also sell things like greetings cards and art sets (containing pencils, ruler and other stationery). The artist studio space has several big tables in two main areas, a conference room, office and quiet space. The ceiling is high and accommodates a mezzanine gallery for artwork storage, with artwork all around the walls.

To one side of Creativity Explored is 'Super 7', a collectables (action figures) store, and on the other side is a barber shop.

On Monday to Friday, the studios are used by artists with developmental disabilities. On Saturdays they have an open-to-all art activity. They invite some of their artists to come and participate so that people with and without developmental disabilities will be able to spend time together.

Meeting Pilar

I was welcomed in to Creativity Explored by Pilar Olabarria, service co-ordinator. She has long flowing hair, pink thick-rimmed stylish glasses, a red apron, a huge warm smile, and warm welcoming energy. Pilar has worked for Creativity Explored for 30 years; she is an artist too. She is clearly passionate about the artists and their work at the studio.

How is Creativity Explored funded?

Overheads (studio space, support staff, etc.) are partly paid for by the local regional centre. (Regional centres are a California-wide network of centres that are involved with enabling people to get support, and are funded by the local government.) The rest of the money comes from commissions and other art sales, and also from grants.

About the artists

Artists range in age from 19 to 60, and differ in how many days a week they spend at the studio. Some do not speak, some do not speak English, and some need a lot of support whilst others are quite independent. On the day I visited, Pilar was setting up an art activity to give artists the opportunity to try painting on a big space, as many of the artists like to work in very small detail, like working with embroidery. After the activity they can go back to their embroidery if they choose to. Each artist has their own way of expressing themselves and there is a stimulating range of materials for those who would like to try something new. It was clear from talking to the artists that they all felt valued.

The artists are supported by teachers who help them explore their chosen medium or whatever they want to do. For example, if an artist enjoys drawing but doesn't use many darker tones, the teacher might introduce the idea of darker tones; however, it's the artist's choice if they want to work with this suggestion.

Adi, an autistic artist, comes to the studio two days a week, and on three other days goes to The Arc (The Arc is a nationwide not-for-profit (charity), providing services for adults and children with learning disabilities/intellectual disabilities and/or autistic people). At The Arc Adi does different classes in subjects like drama and music. Adi is passionate about fashion and one day would like to be a rapper.

Vincent has been at the studio for over 30 years. He makes a range of art, and on my visit, he was making two abstract pieces.

Brian, who is in his twenties, is full of humour and catchphrases. He likes to make art inspired by comic-book characters.

The teachers

If you are not in the arts industry you may be thinking on first glance that 'teachers' sounds a bit patronising. Many people with developmental disabilities find access to mainstream education such as art classes, books, galleries and websites difficult. Information needs to be adapted to their needs, so that they can further explore things that interest them. The word 'teacher' perhaps makes you imagine someone telling people what to do, but the teachers are more like facilitators, helping artists to explore themselves and increase their skills in their chosen mediums. All professional artists continue to learn new skills and get better. If you look at most famous artists, the art they created at the start of their career often looks very different to what they were creating at the end of their career. The teachers at Creativity Explored help to give artists with developmental disabilities a better chance.

Selling artworks

Artists sell their work in the Creativity Explored gallery, and sometimes at shows mainly across the USA. The price varies from US$50 to US$1500 (£38–£1147). Creativity Explored offers a 50/50 split of money received from artwork sales. On the outside this may seem unfair, but Creativity Explored offer much more than just the teaching. Their gallery space is within a trendy part of San Francisco, with plenty of foot fall. They have up-to-date facilities and also enable artists to progress their careers. Their work is their own and they can take it home, but some artists choose to donate their work to Creativity Explored. Other artists and their families request that any profits go to Creativity Explored, so that they don't have an income that they would need to declare to government agencies, which might also affect their benefits.

One recent development is sending artists to mainstream studio spaces to work so that people are not so segregated.

Can this kind of project work in areas other than art?
There are similar projects to Creativity Explored in other areas
of creative practice, and within other industries, such as
horticulture and drama.

Alex's Assistance

You've heard of personal assistants (PAs) who do admin tasks,
for example typing up notes. Well, there are also assistants
who can do errands, pick up gifts, and so on. Alex is one of
those assistants.

Alex is in his early thirties. He lives in an annex attached to
his parents' house. He likes bowling and music, and also really
likes to be around people.

Alex is nonverbal and he has cerebral palsy. He uses PECS
(Picture Exchange Communication System) to communicate.
He studied in college for five years doing art history.

I wanted to include Alex's story because he is someone who
has significant needs but has utilised his care services to run
a business, and I think this could be an important example of
what is possible for many families of adults who need a lot of
support.

Alex needs 24-hour care, and he has support staff
work with him in three shifts each day. He did a few work
experiences, but his family wanted to help him find something
he really enjoyed doing.

Alex is someone who loves to shop! A few years ago,
someone suggested that Alex could start a business doing
errands for people, choosing greetings cards and gifts, or
picking things up from the store/shop. This was a successful
idea – in fact last Christmas he got too busy, so his schedule
needs to be managed.

He has a website and a Facebook page as well as e-mail,

and people also know about him via word of mouth. When people contact him his support workers read the messages to him.

Early on he was part of a youth collective (although he was slightly older than everyone else, they were happy to help). The collective is a city-funded project in St Albert, Canada, which includes low-cost retail space, business training and the opportunity to meet other self-employed people.

Ellen, his mum, wants to work towards not having to coordinate tasks, as Alex's staff are not all in at the same time. She has found the Business Licensing Department in St Albert to be very helpful. Alex's support is paid for via Assured Income for the Severely Handicapped (AISH). Each province within Canada has something like AISH.

During the COVID-19 pandemic, Alex had to stop doing shopping errands for people. However, as his mum writes, 'He started posting positive messages on mailboxes in his sister's neighbourhood and this made us think up a new business for him. He now makes handcrafted cards. His staff help him work hand-over-hand to cut, glue, paint, etc. He charges so that he can buy more supplies.'

Edmonton (Canada) Focus Group

In Edmonton I was very fortunate to have had help to run a focus group. A focus group is where people talk about a particular issue, in this case self-employment. I describe here some of the people in the group.

Made by Brad

Brad is a young man whose mum Debbie helps him run his business Made by Brad. Debbie says that it was her husband who started the business: 'I would be too nervous if it had been up to me.' Brad's day programme had been struggling to support him. 'He would learn the codes for the office doors, and staff started to refuse to go in the office when he was there,' Debbie says.

Brad needs to be busy. He has always enjoyed building things. As a child he enjoyed building Lego models, then the family started buying flat-pack furniture and he enjoyed building that too. His family got to the point where they no longer needed any more new furniture.

Excel Society, a not-for-profit supporting adults with disabilities in Alberta, were running regular sessions at Brad's day programme. One of the people involved was called Ben (of the Think Jar Collective). Brad's dad, Mark, paid for some consultancy with Ben and together they came up with an idea. Mikey Hamm, a local film maker, made a video about Brad which told how he was looking for people with flat-pack furniture that needed to be put together.

Ben was able to work with staff at the day programme so that staff from the programme could take him to a client's house and he would build their furniture. Debbie helps Mark manage Brad's schedule carefully – too much work can definitely be a bad thing. If Brad's schedule gets too busy, he uses sign language to ask for the library, says his mum. Brad charges the minimum wage to clients, which at the time of writing was C$15 an hour.

Anthony at Your Service

Anthony has an intellectual disability and is autistic. Deb, Anthony's mum, wanted to find him something to do that he would enjoy. Anthony doesn't like to be in any one place for a length of time. He is sociable and likes people, and he likes helping people, so she and his support workers came up with the idea of a delivery service. I asked if this was like Uber Eats, and his support worker Jessie told me, 'Uber Eats is more for one-off things. We tend to do regular deliveries.' He has done deliveries for all kinds of things, like giving bags to people at conferences, and care packs for people who have run marathons. They started to get offers of work that needed to be done at times when Anthony didn't have support, so they opened up the opportunity to others with disabilities and now have several teams doing deliveries.

The business has now been expanded to nearby Calgary, and an app has been developed to help manage tasks.

Roma

Roma has two sons, Ben (30) and Grant (28). Both are autistic and have intellectual disabilities. As they reached the end of school, Roma didn't want them to be 'squirreled away in a corner of a basement in front of a TV'. Roma found mentors for her sons doing things they enjoyed.

Ben enjoys pressing buttons and taking photos, and Grant likes to paint. Whilst both sell their work, it's not about profit. everything goes into making more art. Roma says that having mentors was vital; they have come in the form of local students and artists, who are paid for this support.

Dave

Dave works for an organisation called Prospect Human Services, which supports disabled people, including autistic people, to become self-employed (I realise that not all autistic people also identify as disabled). One of Dave's clients, Reginald, came as well.

Reginald

Reginald runs a business called Freaking Awesome T-Shirts.

Reginald said he benefits from someone helping him to learn the skills he needed. As an example, he said that he had recently learned during introductions at a networking event that if someone said something of interest to him, he needed to wait until it was his turn to speak again. These kinds of social skills are often easily learnt by non-autistic people, but for autistic people can be much harder to understand.

Reginald says that Prospect (https://prospectnow.ca), the organisation that has been supporting him with his self-employment, 'can tell you which way is up when it feels like the world around you is collapsing and you're drowning, and that in itself is valuable...cos sometimes I don't know what I should do next. It's overwhelming.'

I am very grateful to Renate Burwash and Gateway in Edmonton for arranging this focus group, hosting me and helping me so much. Thank you and thank you to all the participants. Apart from Reginald's business, none of the participants were focused on making money.

Kindling Studios

Kindling Studios is a project that is run by IGNITE Collective, Inc., a not-for-profit (charity) that runs different projects for people with developmental disabilities (in the USA this includes autistic people). The studio is a working art studio within an art studio centre, Studio Channel Islands, based in Camarillo, California.

The Studio Channel Islands studios used to be a school, but now the former classrooms are rented out by artists. The green spaces have swings and hanging artworks and picnic benches in the 'courtyard'; it's a very collaborative space with artists helping each other out.

To begin with, Kindling Studio artists were not welcomed by some of the other artists who rent out some of the other studios. They would complain about them making too much noise, but Jessie, who is Project Coordinator, has a tattooed chest and wouldn't let anyone mess with her. Fellow artists pointed out that they don't complain about the noise the other artists were making, and everyone has a right to be here. The artists who complained left, but new ones moved in and the other artists are supportive, kind and friendly.

I asked Jessie how the management of Studio Channel Islands felt. She said they were fully supportive, had raised funds for Kindling Studios' rent at their annual gala, and always include the artists in their events.

Kindling Studios has two or three interns and volunteers who come from university volunteering programmes or are just interested, and have community volunteers as well, local artists who teach about art mediums such as quilting, weaving, animation or painting.

About the artists

Alan showed me his portraits and how his style had changed. Jessie explained that she is not a painter, but she is a make-up artist, and so she was able to help Alan learn how to paint contours. His work has changed a lot and he is happy with his progress. For Alan this is way of impressing girls and paying for dates.

I also met David, who speaks very little but paints very detailed portraits of dogs. His work is displayed at a local pizzeria and in two doctors' offices.

Lee sits in his own space. On the wall above him are highly detailed paintings he has done. He looks things up on Google Images and then draws and paints them. He has a passion for car number plates, and draws many of them. (In the USA each state has its name and picture in the number plate the car was registered in.)

Caroline was working on tie dye tote bags and T-shirts, and Esmay was in her second week and was painting a person.

Kindling Studios has three goals for their artists:

- Art
- Entrepreneur
- Personal

They want to help people become artists and do what they want to do with art. They also want them to be able to manage the business side of things, like taking photos for their online store, inventory and tax, and they want people to spend time together, have meaningful relationships and support one another.

Stutterking Bakery

Matt Cottle lives in Phoenix, Arizona; his house has cactuses growing outside.

Matt likes to cook and was inspired by TV programmes, but he found that cooking courses went too fast for him. Through a local not-for-profit SARRC (Southwest Autism Research and Resource Center), he was put in touch with a support worker who was also a pastry chef, who started teaching Matt different recipes. SARRC paid Matt to provide catering at some of their events. People heard about Matt's skills, and now his goods are sold at a country club and a cafe. Currently Matt sells his goods at a farmer's market on a Saturday. He describes this as hard work, and says he doesn't get paid much. He is going to get a part-time job in a cafe to learn how it works, so in the future he can have his own cafe and culinary school.

John's Crazy Socks

John is not autistic, but he does have Down Syndrome, and there are lots of people who are autistic and who have a learning disability like Down Syndrome. I wanted to include his story because it's a good example of setting up a business with your parent and working together.

The Crazy Socks office is in Melville, New York, on Long Island. The building is brightly coloured inside, with orange and blue walls, and welcome mats that have John's picture and say 'John's Crazy Socks'.

John's dad, Mark, was suddenly made unemployed in 2016. John was about to turn 21, which would mean he would no longer be able to attend school because he would have to access adult services. John suggested to his dad they could start a business together. John's first idea was a fun store but they didn't know what this meant. John's next idea was a food truck, but neither John nor Mark knew how to cook. John's third idea was to sell socks. Mark started calling suppliers to buy some socks, but it was hard to find a company willing to sell to people who didn't have a store already. But finally, they found one and John picked out the socks he wanted to sell.

Mark describes their business as a social enterprise because 5% of their profits go to the Special Olympics, and their Awareness Socks raise money for other charitable organisations.

The Special Olympics is an organisation that works worldwide to enable people with learning disabilities to be able to take part in sports, and have their own international Olympic Games. John is a medal-winning athlete with the Special Olympics.

They decided they would like to do something for World

Down's Syndrome Day on 21st March, and looked for a Down Syndrome awareness sock, but there wasn't one. So John designed one and they found a manufacturer to make it happen. They have various other awareness socks which they use to raise funds for charities/not-for-profits.

In the first week of their business they got 42 orders. John wrote personalised thank you notes, and Mark drove John to hand-deliver the orders. People started to share photos on social media about John's socks, and the business grew. One hurdle they had was rapid growth when they got media attention, followed by a slowdown of growth. They employ individuals with differing abilities who are ready, willing and able to work, and more than one-half of their employees have a differing ability. John's Crazy Socks is a unified workplace where everyone works to fulfil the mission to Spread Happiness.

Shane the web developer

Shane develops websites for small businesses.

Shane is in his forties. He has a partner and two kids. Shane changes his hair colour a lot. Currently it is purple, blue and green. As a child his family worried about him spending too much time playing computer games. He quickly learnt to reprogram the games he was playing, and played pranks on his brother like turning the game upside down or making the characters say funny things. Shane says, 'School was as expected for someone who liked all those things. My parents sent me to a sport-obsessed high school. Bad choice in hindsight, but they did their best.' He left school early to go to a technical college, but left 18 months before the end of his course and went to university to study physics. He didn't do the last six months of his course because he struggled with social anxiety. Even getting on a bus became impossible. In all of these education institutions, Shane found the sensory environment a huge barrier.

Shane did his first paid job as a web developer at the age of 17. His client came via his dad, who runs a construction company. He tried different jobs as a young man, like working in a game/movie rental store, but by his early twenties he knew that he needed to make his own job, because he needed to have greater control of his sensory environment.

His work comes from referrals from previous clients, and the business has grown steadily over the last 20 years. He found communication with clients difficult at first; because he works in IT, most communication is via e-mail. He says he naturally communicates in a formal style, but needed to learn how to interpret clients' wants. For example, if they said they wanted a website like a competitor's and he designed something that looked exactly the same, the customer would say they wanted something unique to them.

Shane says, 'There was a phase I went through when I was low on confidence and trying to work out all the social complexities of business relationships. I copied what I figured other people were doing. I always found it a very uncomfortable thing to do, and I stopped doing it after a while. It didn't feel right. After my diagnosis and that of my daughter, I am now completely up front. Masks down and all that.'

He went to the library and read books about communication, and he also listens to a lot of podcasts about IT and business. Perhaps unsurprisingly, there are a lot of people in the IT industry who need help with 'soft skills' (communication, presentations, etc.) and so there are plenty of podcasts about this.

I know a lot of parents worry about their teenage children spending too much time playing games. I asked Shane what his advice would be for these parents. He said, 'Ask your kids what they like about the games they play. Do they like the story? The characters? The artwork? The challenges?' For example, his daughter stumbled upon an online game with robots, but he watched her play the game and found that she was finding the robots and playing with them as if it were a dolls house. His daughter still plays the game, and his partner has an account and joins her sometimes.

Leith: Aspiehelp

Leith McMurray is in her seventies, lives in New Zealand and is the cofounder of Aspiehelp.

'I finished my first degree in my thirties, and then completed a two-year Postgraduate Diploma in Social Work – with difficulty as I had no prior experience.

'After attending a national conference, it was clear to me that, while there was some supportive work being done for children, there was little to none for older people, especially in middle age like me, and no prospect of anyone stepping up. With my social work qualification and an aspie friend with special needs teaching experience, I set up the first support/ counselling organisation for autistic older adults.

'At first we didn't charge for our services. We hoped to pay our rent by donations and grants, but this was not very secure. We therefore brought in fees, and found this definitely produced better attitudes from our clients! We have only recently been able to contemplate paying a wage to our main counsellor as it seems that, after ten years, we now carry recognition and approval from our donors. I do believe we have a valuable contribution to make based on our core values and training.

'Recently autism support organisations have made much

progress in offering very valuable help to families, but still are not government funded. Education and justice use our services but do not offer any payment, nor is there any provision for that.

'I have begun to write a book on the Aspiehelp method of counselling older people, and hope that will be successful. I believe what we all need is for more of our own people to commit themselves to social-work-based support for our folk.'

Wenn Lawson

Wenn is a researcher and psychologist. He is autistic, and earlier in his life was sent to psychiatric institutions. Since 1993 Wenn has run a business, and is now known all over the world. Wenn has written many books, so I've not written much here. I would highly recommend seeking his work out.

Greg the handyman

Greg is a semi-retired handyman, self-employed for about 20 years. He lives with his partner in Marin County, California. Greg is thin and wears thin glasses. He has short hair and is cleanly shaven. He practises Zen Buddhism.

At the start of his working life Greg worked as a research associate in labs in biological sciences; then he started computer programming for vision research. Greg says that neither job was socially sustainable for him: he felt constantly isolated from co-workers. After leaving that work, he spent ten years living on one-twentieth of the prevailing local per capita income, exploring spiritually, and doing a lot of writing. Then he began doing a few jobs as a handyman.

Greg is very good at mechanical thinking and used this

to his advantage. He started serious handyman work by offering his services at very low rates to a friend, helping him renovate his house, and over time Greg developed the confidence that this was something he could do professionally.

Being a handyman meant that he had a lot of control over his social life. He could interact with his clients or not, and it helped him feel less socially isolated. He loves the variety: he is almost always doing something different. By contrast, an autistic friend of Greg's does paint jobs and likes doing repetitive work – which demonstrates how different autistic people can be.

Greg doesn't work full time and wouldn't want to. 'A single big house could keep one person employed full time,' he says, 'but that wasn't the kind of work I wanted to do.' He prefers short jobs, and different kinds of jobs. He does a wide range of jobs, like retro-fitting houses so they will cope with earthquakes, diagnosing and fixing computer problems, putting up shelving, fixing plumbing, installing electrical fixtures, repairing appliances, fixing broken furniture...the list goes on.

Greg normally takes the bus and has found that 'if you wrap construction materials up to look like a present and stick a bow on it the bus driver will let you on... I got two big tables on the bus that way one time,' he says with a chuckle.

Greg practises Zen meditation and says that when he is working he isn't just paying the rent but 'trying to treat the universe and the people in it well'. He tries to offer quality and integrity, and is very honest about paying taxes.

An obvious concern for self-employed people in the USA is healthcare. Years ago, Greg used the San Francisco public health system and highly recommends it: 'It saved my life from cancer years ago. Everything since then has been a flat-out gift!' He says, 'I have done jobs that have scared me, and that have required all my resources intellectually and physically to perform.'

Greg has only marketed his services once, with a poster – which did land him a job caring for a big old house and kept him employed for months. He says that if he wanted his business to grow, he would tell his customers he was looking for more work. (If you are in this situation maybe you could say, 'Please let your friends know about my work as I'd be happy to have more customers.')

Greg advises other autistic people to work out what they are good at and enjoy doing. 'Start small if you can and start with friends as your customers. Do the paperwork from the beginning so you can see if it can be a business that can pay your bills.' Greg says that sometimes you think customers have forgotten you, 'But then the phone rings and you're back in business!' He advises not spending your money when you have plenty coming in, but to save it for when you have fewer customers.

Robyn

Things Robyn did that didn't work

1. Aged 16, I had a business called Robyn's Rodents. I sold computer peripherals like computer mice, keyboards and printers. Initially I got a few sales just before Christmas. After Christmas, sales stopped, and that was the end of that. I can see in hindsight that I needed to talk to my customers more, find opportunities to get myself in front of them, and ask what kinds of computer-related problems they needed solving. Basically, **I needed to learn to understand my customers** at a deeper level. **I needed to adapt to change**, in this case the change was that it was no longer coming up to Christmas.

2. I resigned from a prestigious contract because the culture made me unhappy. I felt I was not genuinely being listened to. I knew that that amount of stress was impacting on my enjoyment of life in general, as well as my other work. I should never have accepted the position in the first place, because I kind of knew that it would involve a lot of bureaucracy and I'm not into that. I had a gut feeling when I was first invited to the role but didn't listen.

I learned that you should listen to your intuition.

3. I was working for a big client, and whilst the work itself was fine and the feedback I got was excellent and consistent, I was finding the paperwork side of the work very difficult. I found that the client did not communicate with me in a way that made it easy for me, so I started paying someone to help me manage the communication and at times translate it from non-literal to literal information. Sarah Jane, who helps me with this, knows I hate e-mail. We don't chat at all via e-mail – no 'How are you?'s. We do all that over the phone. We use e-mails as transactions – for example:

R: Please can you send me the dates for next month?

SJ: Here you go (in a neat table).

It's not that I don't care how Sarah Jane is, it's just that text-based communication is hard for me to process, so I only want the information I need – no more, no less. Now I can take on any client without fearing the communication barriers.

I needed to be OK about paying someone to help me with clients. I was worried about the cost, but customers prefer it as it takes them less time.

4. Moving to cloud-based bookkeeping. My mum used to

do my bookkeeping as I struggled to keep track of invoices (occasionally sending the wrong invoice to the wrong person), and my receipts were screwed up in my wallet, but to move online I had to argue with my parents. I stood my ground, but I wish I could have handled this better. Although I asked for help when writing the e-mail to my mum explaining my plan, she and my dad were still upset about it.

An area for self-development would be conflict resolution.

5. When my first book came out, I organised and did a five-and-a-half-week tour of the UK. This went well, except I lost my voice. I overdid it, and should have taken things slower.

I need to pace myself.

6. Towards the end of my first book tour, I learnt how important managing cash flow is, when I was at a hotel and had maxed out my credit card. I managed to call my bank and negotiate a raise in my credit limit as a fix, but I had very little cash, which panicked me.

Why didn't I have a lot of cash?

Because people hadn't paid me yet. Because it takes 30 days for an invoice to be paid.

I learnt what cash flow was, and how to avoid running out of cash. Previous to this I wouldn't have sought as much credit as I could get as a back-up.

7. I applied for countless arts fundings before I got accepted. I was really put off the first few times, but now I know that is just a thing that happens.

Don't take rejection personally.

8. I've had a few problems with not understanding written communication (it's why I hate e-mail, as I'm worried I'll misunderstand it). On one occasion I thought I had cancelled an account with a supplier, but I hadn't, and then I got a letter from a debt collecting agency. I'd been reluctant to call them as it was an expensive phone number.

I learnt from this that **I need to ask someone else to read over written communication**. I rely on the patterns of the letters rather than their content. If I wasn't expecting it, I am suspicious and will ask for help. I know you might be thinking, 'But you write books.' Yes, but I know what I mean to say, and work with people who support my vision. The start of any written project always involves lots of conversations about my vision for it. I also use a screen reader.

9. I have always loved music, but I didn't pursue music as a career as I didn't know it was possible to make money from music without being a famous musician. When I got to 29, I started to put a lot more effort in. **Four years later a lot of my income comes from creative projects.**

Attributes I think help self-employed people
I think you will find self-employment easier if you can learn to do the following:

- **Lead confidently:** Making the decision about my bookkeeping, or to spend more hours on music, or to make a homemade spaceship on a stage were all things other people doubted would work or be good ideas, but they all worked. You are the one steering your business.
- **Fake it till you make it:** You might not feel confident on the inside, but try to look it on the outside.
- **Listen and respond to feedback** from customers and other people.
- **Research:** Make decisions based on research, and not just on whether other people think something is a good

idea or not (particularly if those people won't be directly affected).

- **Ignore unhelpful information:** I still hear my dad's voice in my head telling me 'You'll get in a muddle' when I went digital with my bookkeeping, but so far, I've not got myself in any muddles.
- **Be agile:** Be willing to change. Change might seem scary, but in life you only go forward – you can't go back in time (at least you can't yet!).
- **Think ahead:** What might happen tomorrow, next month, next year, in three years? Assess and take risks where necessary. Nothing stays the same forever.
- **Believe in yourself.**
- **Have multiple revenue streams.**
- **Don't be scared of failure:** Sometimes you'll try something, and it won't work. This happens to everyone. Learn from what didn't work, adapt, and then try again.

Answers to Bookkeeping Activity

Here are the answers to the Bookkeeping Activity from the end of Chapter 17.

Income

Date	Item	Payment method	Amount	Quantity	Total £
	T-shirt local band	card	£25	7	175
	T-shirt local band	cash	£25	7	175
	T-shirt Blue Sky Thinking	card	£30	20	600
	T-shirt Motorbike	cash	£12	30	360
20/06/20	Shipping costs paid		£30	1	30
Total £					1340

Expenses

Date	Item	Payment method	Quantity	Unit price	Cost £
02/06/20	Plain T-shirts	card	100	3	300
11/06/20	Water				25
10/07/20	Electricity				80
01/06/20	Inks				50
07/06/20	Phone				25
	Shipping to customers				30
	Insurance	direct debit			6
Total £					516

Categories

	Stock	Utilities	Shipping	Telecoms	Consumables	Insurance
	300					
			30			
		25				
		80				
				25		
					50	
						6
Total £	300	105	30	25	50	6

by the same author

The Autism-Friendly Guide to Periods

This is a detailed guide for young people aged 9 to 16 on the basics of menstruation. Created in consultation with young people, an online survey and a group of medical professionals, this is a book that teaches all people about periods, which can be a scary and overwhelming issue.

Promoting the fact that everyone either has periods or knows someone who does, the book reduces the anxiety girls face in asking for help. It offers

direct advice on what periods look and feel like and how to manage hygiene and pain. It also breaks up information using flaps and step-by-step photos of how to change pads and tampons, it discusses alternatives to tampons and pads, and gives information about possible sensory issues for people with autism.

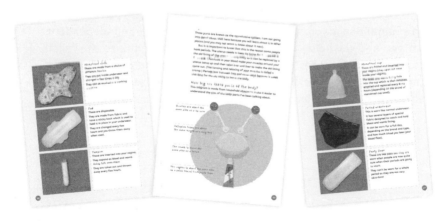

£12.99 | $18.95 | HB | 96pp | ISBN 978 1 78592 324 1 | eISBN 978 1 78450 637 7

The Independent Woman's Handbook for Super Safe Living on the Autistic Spectrum

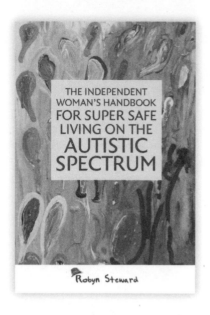

Certain characteristics of autism, such as difficulty understanding social cues, may make women vulnerable to potentially dangerous situations. Robyn Steward has written this supportive guide to help all women on the autistic spectrum live independently, make their own choices in life, and be safe whilst doing so.

This book will provide you with the knowledge to recognise potential risks to your personal safety and the skills and strategies required to avoid and overcome them. Informed by a survey of, and interviews with, women on and off the autistic spectrum, it explores common safety issues encountered by women and offers practical advice to help you stay safe and supported in your independence. Topics covered include friendships, relationships and sex, alcohol and drugs, money and employment and staying safe outside the home and online.

This handbook is your guide to super safe living as an independent woman and will help you to stay safe whilst living life to the full. It may also be of interest to your family, friends and carers, giving them insight into life on the spectrum and confidence that you will enjoy your independence in an informed and safe manner.

£13.99 | $19.95 | PB | 376pp | ISBN 978 1 84905 399 0 | eISBN 978 0 85700 765 0